UNDERCOVER AGAIN - Fighting Human Trafficking

UNDERCOVER AGAIN - Fighting Human Trafficking

Bob Ojala

A3Pi Services, LLC

CONTENTS

1. Author's Note — 1
2. Lover's Quarrel — 4
3. History — 9
4. Liz - Snooping — 28
5. Liz - Meddling — 42
6. Looking Sleazy — 54
7. Asian Imports — 62
8. Tiffany's Story — 70
9. Caught in the Act — 74
10. Burt Snyder — 83
11. Liz - Photoshoot — 89

CONTENTS

12 | Major Sting 97

13 | Majestic Modeling 107

14 | Burt - Hendrickson Pay-Back 120

15 | The China Story 130

16 | Burt - Devious Plan 136

17 | Liz and Lenny 148

18 | Laurie Meets Lenny 163

19 | District Attorney's Office 172

20 | Lenny 177

21 | Liz - The China Solution 190

22 | Burt's Apology 198

23 | Burt - Nosing Around 204

24 | Herb - Hunting 216

25 | Burt - On the Tail 226

26 | Closing the Fake Daycare 236

CONTENTS

27 ▍ Elisa Jandra **244**

28 ▍ Liz & Steve **247**

ABOUT THE AUTHOR **253**

© 2023 by Bob Ojaka. All rights reserved. No portion of this book may be reproduced, stored in a retrieval system, or transmitted in any form or by any means—electronic, mechanical, photocopy, recording, scanning, or other— except for brief quotations in critical reviews or articles, without the prior written permission of the publisher.

1

Author's Note

My novels are always **stand-alone**. I am not a fan of book series that leave you hanging, with unanswered questions at the end of one book, requiring you to buy the next book to see what happens. My stories do have main characters you'll see from one novel to the next. For instance, if you like Steve in this book, you can meet him as a 12-year-old in *"A Tugboater's Life."* Or follow Steve's parents' growing family in *"The Tugboater's Family"* and *"Crew's Ship Affairs."* If you also want to know how Steve and Liz got together, you will love their story in *"KIDNAPPED – A Tugboater's Tale."* Just know that you can enjoy each story without reading the one before.

I tend to write about "what I know." This is something learned from Stephen King's book, *"On Writing."* So, having spent 45 years working with ships, ships' crews, and shipyards, my stories are based on events surrounding these areas since that's what I know best.

But what about human trafficking, you might be wondering....

Well, in addition to working with ships, ships' crews, and shipyards, I also worked for the U.S. Army Corps of Engineers for seven years, during a recent recession when my marine consulting business was slow. I remember my boss once told me during my first year there that I had to attend a training session the next morning on Human Trafficking Awareness. The Corps of Engineers is primarily made up of civilian employees, but we all had to take the same training as active-duty Army personnel. At the time, I thought the training was stupid, after all, human trafficking only occurs in Third World countries.

I was shocked to find out that this was not true! Human trafficking is worse in the United States than it is anywhere else in the world. Today, that may be rivaled by traffickers abducting children at the Ukraine border. But the reality is that many Americans still believe that trafficking, even if it occurs in the United States, only occurs in the ghettos of large cities like New York, Chicago, and Detroit.

According to case studies presented as part of the U.S. Corps of Engineers training videos, most human trafficking cases can be found in small Midwestern towns. And contrary to what people think, not all victims of human trafficking are runaway girls looking to have a good time by selling their bodies for sex. In fact, about 13% of trafficked victims are male. And even though not all victims are used for sex, the majority are raped, and the average age is thirteen. Girls as young as ten are sold for sex after being abducted.

In March 2022, a retired Cook County (Chicago) judge was among more than 100 people arrested in a human-trafficking-for-sex sting. Over 150 girls, ranging in age from 13-17 years old, were rescued during that operation. Imagine that! And in a recent FBI sting in Wisconsin, over 150 adults were arrested for abducting children as young as 12 years old.

While I cannot stop human trafficking from happening, I am hoping to at least raise awareness of its existence and dangers through my books/stories. I also hope that through my stories, parents will be prompted to listen to their children and to love and protect them from becoming victims of these crimes. These crimes can happen to anyone regardless of age, ethnicity, race, or gender. The threat is real...

2

Lover's Quarrel

UNDERCOVER AGAIN
Fighting Human Trafficking

"Liz, you promised! You told me when you went back to Law School that you were leaving that undercover stuff behind. You damn near got killed within the first week I knew you. Now that you've made me fall in love with you, I'm not going to let you get killed," Steve said, pacing the dust-free floor of their apartment in Erie. Liz was still standing by the door. Steve stopped to look at her and shook his head. They had just come home from a nice dinner at their favorite Italian restaurant, where the discussion about Liz's plans had started.

"Wait just a minute there, Stevie boy!" Liz shot back at Steve. "You were the one who ogled me with those loving, baby blues. I had to beat you off with a stick...actually with a two-by-four if I remember."

Steve rubbed his hand across his face as if trying to wipe away the smile that threatened to appear at the memory of how they had met.

He had met Liz Trent a little over three years ago when she was working with the Kentucky State Police as an undercover investigator in their sex-offenders detail. Steve was working on one of his uncle's tugboats for the summer when two of the crewmembers, a husband and wife, went missing after they went into town to pick up some pizzas. That case led to a string of operations that eventually led to Steve meeting Liz when she was introduced as part of an undercover sting operation set to bust a '*stable*' of trafficked young girls.

"What are you being talked into this time, Babe?" Steve asked Liz. "I'm not sure that undercover police work fits into the work description of a lawyer who just passed the bar. Seriously, Liz! You lived too close to the edge back then. I thought you'd put that life behind you. Now you've got me scared again."

Liz walked to Steve and stood before him. "First of all, I took a Leave of Absence. I can't do this as part of the District Attorney's office. I'll be more careful this time, Steve," she said, cupping his face in her hands. "The County Prosecutor is working a case with a family whose young daughter was abducted and raped. One of her classmates turned up dead. and we think they were abducted together. We don't have the hard evidence to make any convictions. I know I can get it done."

Steve stepped out of Liz's grasp.

"The other prosecutors don't have the first-hand experience

that I have to make the traffickers hang themselves," Liz said, "figuratively speaking."

"Yeah, I know how you work. But even with a good team backing you up last time, they lost you during the transport. You spent three days being injected with drugs in that lovely butt of yours; that was really dangerous. Even you said you were lucky to have survived the overdoses. And now you're freelancing, without backup?"

"Steve, I've met the girl they abducted. She's thirteen now, only twelve at the time, and she's been drugged and raped for three months. One of the guys who paid to use her suddenly got a dose of conscience and helped her escape, but he's too scared to testify or even tell us where he found her. And you know how these stable operators can talk themselves out of trouble. I want to get these guys, Steve. I can't let them get away with this."

When Steve first met Liz, she was introduced as a Kentucky State policewoman and a sex crimes investigator. She looked like some 17-year-old kid because she looked younger than her age. Steve was immediately attracted to her good looks, but he thought Liz was too young for him. He later found out that Liz was twenty-seven, which still posed a bit of a problem since he was two months away from his 21st birthday and about to start his senior year in college. Even so, they felt a strong attraction to each other and started dating not very long afterwards.

Steve had seen Liz in action as an undercover agent and even witnessed her passion for rescuing young women and boys who had been kidnapped by traffickers. She cried with the abductees she rescued, helped to get them counseling, and got indescribable highs when she caught and helped to convict "the perps," as she called them. The trouble was, those emotional rollercoasters... the highs, and lows, mixed with the dangers of working as an undercover victim were seriously affecting Liz's health. It was physically and emotionally shocking to her system, not to mention that she could be murdered if she were found out.

Steve found all of this disturbing; he didn't want to lose her. He had fallen in love with Liz quickly and, despite Liz's intention to slow down their affair to a crawl, Steve knew that Liz shared those same romantic feelings. Liz needed frequent, long hugs to dispel her emotional lows after experiencing some disturbing episodes in her undercover life. She would then give Steve a passionate kiss, and suddenly pull away, telling Steve he needed to stop her when she kissed him. At first, Steve was confused by Liz's mood swings, but once he began to understand what damage had been done to Liz's psyche, due to her terrible job, Steve knew he needed this complex woman in his life.

But now, three years after Liz's last dangerous 'project' as she called them, and with her new job as a prosecuting attorney, Steve thought that Liz was overcoming the traumas and they could finally have a normal life together. He was ready to start his own career as a consulting Naval Architect and was even ready to ask Liz to marry him. He had delayed leaving Ann Arbor and working for one of his professors so he could be near Liz while she finished her degree. Now, it appeared she wanted to step back three years, into her old, messed-up life.

Steve was studying Naval Architecture at the University of Michigan. Even before she met Steve, Liz had noticed her work with the Kentucky State Police was beginning to affect her emotional health, so she enrolled part-time in Pre-Law classes, hoping to eventually fight these 'perps' in the courtroom instead of on the front lines. When Liz saw the mutual attraction between her and Steve, she decided to leave the Police and enroll full-time in the U-of-M's Law School, to see if she and Steve were a good match.

Steve, on the other hand, was hopeful that Liz's Law Degree meant she would be safer but as it turns out, she was not done with putting her life in danger for the sake of others. Steve didn't want to see Liz return to those huge emotional swings, and certainly didn't want her to be in physical danger like she had been in the past. Knowing that the woman you love could be killed by one of the criminals she was trying to catch in a sting operation, was more than Steve could live with, in a marriage. Did he love her enough to put up with those circumstances again?

3

History

(Erie, Pennsylvania)
Police are being flooded by a sudden upsurge in young teen runaways, and parents have been screaming for help. Many of the teens, mostly young girls between twelve and sixteen years of age, do not fit the normal profile of a runaway. The two recent cases, both twelve-year-old girls, came from upper-middle-class families with stay-at-home mothers and professional fathers. They had disappeared just two days apart.

After nearly six weeks, one of the girls is found dead in the harbor, near Presque Isle State Park. The girl's body was in the water for several weeks, so the cause of death was not officially determined. However, the autopsy did show that some form of vaginal penetration may have occurred, so an investigation began, mainly questioning the parents. The girl had three sisters and a brother and after the parents agreed to family group counseling, the counselor did not believe that the girl had been abused at home.

Then three months after the two girls' disappearances, the second girl was dropped at a small Emergency Care facility near Erie, just over the Ohio State Line. The man who brought the girl there said he was going out to call the police, but he then disappeared. However, the Ohio State Police were able to locate the man from surveillance videos at the Medical Facility. He refused to give details, only saying he'd seen the girl wandering a back road. He eventually admitted that he had rescued the girl from an abusive situation, but said he was afraid to say where he found her.

It took several days before the traumatized girl finally spoke her name, and the Erie Police were then notified. Medical examinations showed that this girl had been severely damaged by multiple vaginal penetrations. She even had to be sedated in order to be examined. Any time a male entered her room, she became terrified and screamed, "No more!"

This reaction she had to men resulted in an investigation, and the parents of both girls reported that the two girls had been friends. The rescued girl's mother, Stephany Jandra, had two other children, both younger than the victim, and the mother attended counseling with her daughter to determine what had occurred. Using hypnosis, the details of a photo shoot on a boat began to appear, with a man starting to fondle the two girls as he took their pictures. He slowly removed their clothing, telling them the pictures were going to be artistic, showing them pictures he'd taken of other naked girls. Then the man slowly undressed and started using oil on the girls' bodies, eventually penetrating them manually. The Jandra girl said that the man began having sex with her friend, which she had only heard about when the older girls at school described it. Her friend began screaming and the Jandra girl panicked and tried to run away. The man struck her, and she blacked out.

When she woke up, she found herself locked in a room in a very dirty place with about ten other girls. One of the older girls was always giving her a shot, then leading her to a room where a man was waiting. She usually passed out as he abused her, but was always sore and bleeding when she woke up again. The last time, the man in the room didn't hurt her but took her away in his car. She just remembered the man swearing a lot as he drove, and then he took her to a hospital.

The evidence gathered during the hypnosis sessions mentioned a modeling agency, Majestic Modeling. The police investigated Majestic, and surprisingly, the owner recognized the Jandra girl's name and showed them several nice, professional-looking photos he'd taken of the girl. He paid her for allowing him to take sample photographs of her, and he showed the police his records of the cash payment. He said he sold such pictures to retail stores in other states for use in their children's clothing departments. He also said he asked the girl if he could take more pictures, but he needed her parents to sign a release, so he could use her pictures. The girl had told him that she wanted this money to buy a birthday present for her mother and asked him to wait until after her mother's birthday to get her parents' signatures. He agreed, but the girl said she never saw the man again. A young boy from her school had taken her and her friend to the Yacht Club for a photo shoot on a boat out on Lake Erie, and that's where the assault occurred.

The police turned their findings over to the District Attorney's office, saying that they felt Majestic's owner was not telling them everything he knew, even though his story covered all the areas that might have gotten him into hot water.

"He'd certainly heard that the girl was rescued, and he had more than enough time to create these records. If he's responsible for sending those two girls out on that boat, we don't want to close this case, and the girl's parents want him punished," the detective said.

DISTRICT ATTORNEY'S OFFICE

"I don't want to put a 13-year-old girl on the stand using only circumstantial evidence, knowing that her pimp will just lie under oath. We don't even know where this 'dirty place' with other girls is located, and even if we can get her rescuer's testimony, we cannot prove that the pimp actually sold her services to him. He'll just say the customer brought the girl to the motel on his own. You know how that always goes."

Liz was discussing the trafficking case with the District Attorney. A new type of brothel in small Midwest towns was using old, 60's style motels as places of business, and this latest 'stable' operator in Pennsylvania was starting to use very young girls in his brothel. He was charging very high fees and claiming that the girls were virgins who were just getting started in the business. He had used that ploy with the 13-year-old girl in question, for nearly three months, claiming her virginity several times per day. She was rescued when the last man to fall for that story saw how badly abused the girl was. He loaded her into his car and drove her away to safety. They found out later that the man had called the motel and told the pimp that the girl had tried to steal his car and was eventually able to escape. He had taken her to a local health clinic and then anonymously contacted the local police soon afterwards.

The girl was on the missing person list since her disappearance, and once she told the medical staff her name, the police contacted the girl's parents and the Erie Police. The police and the girl's parents brought the case to the District Attorney, Thomas Pierson, for prosecution, after they did a preliminary investigation.

Tom Pierson was a career public servant. He had started as a public defender in Erie County before becoming an Assistant District Attorney. He served as a public defender for five years and eleven as an attorney before the then-district attorney died of a sudden heart attack, and Tom Pierson was asked to fill the vacancy until the next election. He ultimately decided to run as an Independent for the position. At age forty-one, Tom was the youngest District Attorney ever elected to that position in Erie, and he'd now held the job for twelve years. Tom was a well-respected family man with a wife and three teens. He also held several volunteer directorship positions with local charities.

Tom was friendly, his staff liked him, and unlike most lawyers of his time, he let his work speak for him, not his clothes and cars. In fact, he dressed simply and drove an older model van to work.

"So, Mr. Pierson, we're just going to let this guy get away with this?" Liz asked.

"This is why prostitution is seldom prosecuted, Liz," Tom replied. "The customers are ashamed of what they've done, so they refuse to testify. The pimps have no problem lying, and the girls are scared. Do you want to see this 13-year-old on the stand after everything else she's endured? His attorney will find so many holes in her testimony, that it will only be more humiliating to her. And there will be enough doubt that even a good jury will let the pimp walk."

"No. I understand. But this pimp is abusing the young ones. Unlike the guy I witnessed in Flint a few years ago, who controlled his girls with kindness, this goon is beating and drugging his girls. Do you remember the girl who was found dead in the harbor? I'm thinking these two cases may be traced to the same operation."

"I know your history, Liz, and I'm really sorry, but I cannot ask the Sherriff to arrest someone without enough evidence. Other than what the young girl has told us through her counselor, which is all circumstantial, we have nothing. She talked about Majestic Modeling, some guy on a boat, and a motel she couldn't locate for us. We have nothing but a frightened girl's mixed-up memories of three months living in hell."

"Can I ask you a question, Mr. Pierson? I'll tell you upfront that it may sound weird."

"I'm getting used to unusual questions from you, Liz. And I meant that comment to be complimentary, so go ahead."

"Okay, here goes. Do I still look young enough to pass as a teenager?"

Tom Pierson laughed. "I know you aren't hitting on me, Liz. But no, you look like you are an old lady, maybe twenty, even twenty-one."

"Okay. That's close enough. So, now let me ask you, do I still look good enough to be a model?"

"Don't tell me that you're thinking of a career change already? Working with the law isn't quite what you expected?"

"I'm serious, Mr. Pierson, I have an idea."

"Well, seeing this is just you and me talking, please just call me Tom. But what the heck is your idea?"

"Okay, from what we know, the girl said she was approached by a young teenage boy at school who told her she was pretty. He said he knew someone who would pay her to take her picture. That first photo session took place at Majestic Modeling, correct?"

"Yes, but we talked to them, and they admitted they took the girl's picture. They said they paid her $50 and told her she was too young. The owner said he would need her parents' consent to go any further. We had no cause to ask for a search warrant."

"Well, I still think that was the front for the sex trafficking. What do you think, Tom?"

"I agree, but their records show a cash payment to the girl and then nothing. It's hard to find anything incriminating when they admit they took one set of pictures and paid her, and even went on to tell her she needed her parent's signature to take more photos."

"But that's not what the girl has told us. She said she returned for additional pictures. Those additional pictures progressed to becoming nude photos on some boat, and finally to sex. Once the sex started, she was abducted."

"Okay, Liz. We both agree. But his attorney would say that it's a story from a hysterical young girl. And we also don't want to humiliate her on the stand."

"What if we could get testimony from someone on the inside of the agency?"

"We tried that. Nobody is willing to talk."

"I would talk, Tom. I want to get inside Majestic Modeling."

"That takes a lot of time, Liz. How do you plan to do it?"

"Give me a leave of absence, Tom? I don't want you to know exactly what I'm doing, so I can't work in your office while I'm doing this."

"I hate to lose you from my staff, Liz. This is way above and beyond."

"I'll have you talk to my intended husband, Steve Steiner. He can tell you that once my mind is set on something like this, I just can't let it go. And if you do meet him, don't tell him I said he's my intended husband. I need to keep him guessing for a while longer."

"I'm worried, Liz. This might be called entrapment. How can you avoid that pitfall?"

"I guess first of all, I shouldn't talk to you about my detailed plans, Tom. I think I have that figured out, though."

"I must admit, I'd like to see these people pay for what they did to that girl. When do you want to start?"

"Right now sounds good to me, I guess. Then I need to go home and convince Steve that he shouldn't have me put in a straitjacket. I promised the poor guy I'd never do undercover work again."

Before leaving the courthouse complex, Liz went to the adjacent Erie Police station and talked to the desk sergeant. She had gotten to know the desk sergeant from her frequent trips to meet with prisoners and their attorneys. Many of the officers at the station liked Liz because she had a great personality and good looks. Liz asked the Sergeant if she might talk the department out of a few nice 8 x 10 glossies for a special project she was working on, joking that she didn't want them to look like mugshots. The Sergeant made a call and another policeman quickly appeared, with a big smile on his face.

"So, Miss Trent, how can I help you?" the officer asked.

"I have a special project going, which I can't fully discuss, but I need a few nice photos taken of me, with a name, not my true name, done in a fancy-looking font at the bottom. Can you do that? And it's sorta' a rush. I need them before Monday."

"That sounds like a modeling portfolio. Not changing jobs, are ya? We'll miss you," the officer said.

"No, not really. But don't tempt me. There are days I've thought about it," Liz said with a chuckle.

"As long as you promise not to leave us, Miss Trent, I'd be happy to oblige. I have the software to add that name in an appropriate font as well. What name are you going to use in your modeling career?"

Liz could tell the officer was bored and probably having a

good time with this, so, she said, "I was thinking about Trixie Turner, but I don't think I look like a Trixie, do you?

"If you can still use your first name, I think you look more like a Liz Thomas, or maybe a Liz Logan. What do you think?"

"I like sticking with the same initials. Liz Thomas it is. Thanks, Officer Giles."

"Oh, please just call me Jim, seeing I'm launching you into this new career. I won't ask, but I'm real curious about what you're up to."

"Jim, I promise that when I finish this project, I will tell you the whole story."

"Well then, come back to my studio, normally called the Line-Up Room. I guess we'll have to keep the suspect height markers out of the pictures, right?"

"Well, that actually gives me an idea for a couple of interesting pictures," Liz said.

Thirty minutes later, Liz headed home with a promise from Officer Jim Giles that he'd have ten nice glossies ready for Liz Thomas the next morning, in an envelope at the desk sergeant's cubicle.

Liz asked, "How can I repay you, Jim?"

"Just don't forget to tell me what this is all about, whenever you can."

The rest of the weekend with Steve was terrible. She had promised Steve that she would never put her life in danger again, doing undercover police work. She told Steve, "I'm not a policewoman anymore, so I'm not breaking our agreement."

"Damn it, Liz. That's just a technicality, and you know it.

UNDERCOVER AGAIN - FIGHTING HUMAN TRAFFICKING

You're still going undercover to get inside a criminal organization. You're breaking our agreement!"

"But you said you loved me, Steve."

"What does that have to do with it?" Steve asked. He was mad and showing it.

"If you love me, you want me to be happy. And I'm not happy because we cannot prosecute these people who abducted this sweet, 13-year-old girl. You need to let me do this if you want me to be happy, Steve," Liz said. And she was giving Steve her patented pouty look, hoping to get her way.

"So, there's no way I can talk you out of this?" Steve said.

"None. And by the way. I need all the hugs and kisses I can get this weekend because I'm moving out on Monday morning."

"Moving out? Why?" Steve asked, looking very worried.

"My new job on Monday will expect me to be living alone. I'm going to rent a room near the modeling agency. I can't be living with a professional engineer if I'm getting an entry-level modeling job, can I?"

"I hope that's the last bit of shocking news you're throwing at me tonight."

"Just one last shocker, Stevie boy. My boss, Mr. Pierson, told me I looked like an old lady of twenty, maybe even twenty-one."

"And what's wrong with that? You just turned thirty-one last month."

"But remember? My goal was to still get carded when I was forty. It looks like I'm aging faster than expected."

"I think I'm in love with a crazy woman. So, does that mean I won't see you again until you crack this case wide open?"

"Can we sneak to a hotel if I need consoling?" Liz asked.

Steve remembered the several sessions he'd experienced with Liz when she was still with the Kentucky State Police. Her emotions boiled over when she had to break the news to the sister of an abducted girl whose body had been found. The girl, only fourteen, had been killed by a sex trafficker using an overdose of the same animal tranquilizer that nearly killed Liz. Liz took these cases very personally, and from what Steve knew about the case with this local 13-year-old girl and the terrible things that were done to her, he knew that Liz wouldn't rest until she was able to nab the guilty parties. *Love is hell*, Steve thought.

On Monday morning, Liz dressed in a pair of holey jeans and a cut-off T-shirt. Her long blond hair was washed and pulled into a ponytail, using a purple rubber band, the kind used to bundle produce at the grocery store. She figured that made her look the part of a struggling young model. When she was done getting dressed, she packed a small duffel bag. She had developed a very professional look over the last year while working in the D.A.'s office, so she liked to dress casually on weekends. It felt like such a relief.

Liz had already found a rooming house near Majestic Modeling. All she needed now was to find a job, one that would be a great coverup for being a struggling model.

Majestic Modeling Agency was adjacent to a small liquor store, both had rear doors that opened into an alley. The alley was filled with garbage dumpsters and overgrown bushes. Liz took note of this in case she needed an escape in the future. Majestic also had a side driveway that led into the alley. In that driveway, Liz noticed a car and a van parked there. It didn't appear that anyone used the alley entrances for anything other than garbage.

Liz approached the front door. Right before she entered, she heard a buzzer sound in the back room, then footsteps, followed by the appearance of an older man. Liz guessed him to be in his mid-fifties. The front office was sparsely furnished with two old, vinyl-covered lounge chairs and a glass-topped counter. Liz thought it looked like an old dry-cleaning business.

The man came into the front office, smiled, and said, "Well, aren't you a pretty one? How can I help you?"

"I'm new in town," Liz replied. "I'm looking to see if you might have some modeling work. I did some modeling down in Kentucky and West Virginia."

"How old are you, might I ask?"

"I'm going to be twenty-one in a few weeks. I hope that's not too old for the work you have. What type of projects do you handle?" Liz asked.

"No, twenty-one is okay. With the right makeup, you could look younger. We specialize in teen shots, the sweet, innocent stuff, you know? And if our customers want anything special, we try to please."

"Anything special? How do you mean?"

"You know, we've had some customers ask to take nude photos. Nothing raunchy, just the clean artistic nudes, if you know what I mean. Not sure if you might be interested, but those pay a little more."

"Oh," Liz simply said.

She walked a little further and looked around. She felt the man's eyes piercing into her back, studying her.

"If that's a problem, you don't have to do those. We can stick to the sweet, innocent stuff---"

"Oh no!" Liz said, cutting him off before he could finish. "If they're artistic nudes, I'm comfortable with those. I've done nudes before. What rates do you pay? By the hour or by the job?" Liz asked.

"I guess that sorta depends on you, and what you might be willing to do. Each shot comes with its own price tag."

"I see."

"Do you have any samples of your work?" the man asked. Liz thought she heard a hint of suspicion in his voice.

She sat the bag containing her portfolio on the glass countertop and pulled out an 11x14 binder containing shots she had paid a friend to have done just days before.

"Just these from my last job in Kentucky," she said, "no nude shots. They were for a local magazine down there." Liz handed the man the binder. He flipped through the pages, smiling approvingly.

"Those two with those numbers behind you are cute," he finally said, a few pages in. "It looks like you are in a police line-up, and using your hands to form a mask over your eyes. That photographer was very artistic."

"Thank you," Liz said.

"So, I see that your name is Liz Thomas. I like these a lot, Liz."

"I'm glad to hear that," Liz replied.

"I see you're still carrying your bag. Haven't found a place to stay yet?"

"I wanted to find a job first. Don't have much money, so didn't want to commit to renting yet."

"I'll tell you what. I could pay you $40 a day to keep an eye on my shop, just take messages, and so forth, so I can get time out in the field taking photos. Then, if I get some modeling shoots for you, those pay extra. That way, you can pay your rent and have enough for groceries, so you can stick around. I'll leave the tips from my customers up to you, but I'll tell them it is expected."

Just then, a young boy, maybe fifteen, came through the front door. He sounded out of breath and acted excited. "Hi, Mr. Radovich. I think I found that girl you needed. Can I bring her by tomorrow? I think she could use the extra money."

"Yeah, Lenny. Tomorrow is fine."

"After school, okay, Mr. Radovich?"

"Sure thing, Lenny."

"That's great. See you then. How much, Mr. Radovich? $150 like before? This girl is hot!"

"It depends on how she looks, Lenny. The customer wants pictures of her holding a doll, to remind him of his daughter when she was a little girl. If she looks the part, we'll talk about it."

"Okay then. See you after school, Mr. Radovich."

The man turned to Liz after the boy left. "You see the kind of work I get? If I hadn't been here, Lenny might not have brought the girl for this shoot. That's why I could use your help, to answer the phone, take messages and call my cell phone when important things like this happen. And of course, I'll try to find modeling jobs for you."

"Thank you, Mr. Radovich. I appreciate you giving me this job, it will help me to get back on my feet quickly."

"Had problems back home in Kentucky?"

"Yes. My parents didn't like me modeling, and my ex-boyfriend told them I had taken my top off during a shoot and they kicked me out."

"Ahh, I understand. Some parents can be very controlling."

"Thanks. When would you like me here, Mr. Radovich?"

"Let's say, ten to six. Can you start tomorrow?"

"Yes, Mr. Radovich, I could even start today if you need me to."

"No, that's quite alright. I'd like to get the place a little cleaned up before you start, so tomorrow is fine. And call me Rudy."

"Rudy, yes. One more thing," Liz said and then hesitated a bit.

"What is it, Liz?"

"I was wondering if you could pay me in cash. Not having to pay taxes on what I make here would allow me to avoid taxes. I could really use the money."

"That's no problem at all, Liz. I don't much like the paperwork myself. We'll keep your employment on a cash basis. Better for both of us."

Liz was surprised by Rudy Radovich. He didn't look like a typical low-life stable operator. He was well-groomed and acted professionally. She thought he might be coloring his hair to hide some gray. His file showed that he was a Naturalized U.S. Citizen from Bosnia, but he had lost most evidence of an accent, and he spoke good English. Although the young girl said that she had worked for Majestic Modeling and had mentioned the name, Radovich, this was not the person who held her captive in the motel. She had described that man as being much younger, with long hair in a ponytail. Then there was the part about being on a boat, which the girl seemed very confused about. Rudy did not appear to be a yachter.

Liz went back to the rooming house to unpack and get settled. She met her landlady, Mrs. Behrendt in the stairway. She asked Liz if she had found a job yet and Liz said she had.

"Well that was quick, was it the grocery store?"

"No, I actually found a job taking care of the shop at Majestic Modeling."

"Oh," Mrs. Behrendt said. Liz heard a hint of concern in her voice.

"Why, is that not a better job than working at the grocery store," Liz asked her.

"Oh, I'm sure it is. Just be careful around Radovich. None of us in the neighborhood trust him much."

"Why is that Mrs. Behrendt?" Liz asked, hoping to learn more about Radovich.

"Well, I shouldn't be talking bad about someone you just met."

"I think maybe I need to know. I certainly won't tell him

what you tell me. If you're telling me to be careful, I want to know why. I'm going to be working with him, but I also want to feel safe."

"Okay then. But all of us ladies in the neighborhood noticed Radovich looking at all the young girls. Not that most men don't look at pretty girls when they pass, but Radovich has a very lewd look in his eyes when he does. And to make it worse, we notice him giving that same look to the younger girls. I mean those in grade school, like just ten or twelve years old. That just isn't right, you know?"

"Oh my," said Liz. "I'll watch out for him. Thank you for confiding in me."

"You're not going to let him take pictures of you, are you? We wonder what really goes on in his back room."

"I am, that's the job."

Mrs. Behrendt made a face.

"Is there something else you're not saying, Mrs. Behrendt?"

"Oh, no. Just be careful, Liz. I'm sure you can take care of yourself around him. We just don't trust him, that is all.

"Thank you, I'll be careful," Liz said.

Mrs. Behrendt had mentioned a back room, and Liz made a mental note to check out this room in the morning.

Later that night, Liz texted Steve:

"I just wanted to let you know that I have a job at Majestic Modeling, 10-6 each day. I'm working in the front of the shop. I'll be fine, but I'll text or call you every evening to let you know I'm okay. If you don't hear from me by midnight each night, call Mr. Pierson. I'm doing nothing dangerous, but I'll learn a lot about this operation."

Steve texted back almost immediately:

"Call me if anything goes wrong. My phone will be on 24/7. I love you and if you get hurt, I will be very upset with you. You may have to visit me in jail after I take care of anybody who hurts you!"

Liz texted back saying:

"I love you too, Stevie boy! I'll be fine."

Liz had gotten into the habit of calling him 'Stevie boy' because Steve was six years younger than her. When they first met, they were immediately attracted to one another. Steve was looking for a serious woman and Liz was looking for a sincere guy who wouldn't be turned off by her unusual career. She had lost most male admirers early after they heard what Liz did for a living. When Steve's mom heard about this '*older woman*' making eyes at her son, and that this woman dealt with sex trafficking, there were some serious conversations held, before Steve's mom was eventually won over. That was over three years ago, and now Steve's mom kept asking when they were getting married.

4

Liz - Snooping

The next morning, Liz ordered take-out from the corner Deli. She got her favorite avocado toast and an Americano. She was already at the front door when Mr. Radovich showed up. "Punctual little rascal, aren't you? Good to know," he said.

"I sure try to be," Liz said.

"Well, let me show you around a little bit, and then I need to do some running around on jobs for a few hours. I'm glad you'll be here today, so I won't miss any messages."

Radovich showed Liz his phone system and how he wanted her to write down messages. Then he gave her his cell phone number in case something urgent came up. "I have some projects in the back room that I don't want messed with, so stay out of there," he said to Liz.

Liz nodded. She knew she needed to behave as ignorantly as she looked to avoid raising Rudy's suspicions.

"So, you understand what to do?"

"Yes, I do. I assume you have a restroom?" Liz asked.

"Oh, yes. Sorry! That's in the back room. You can go back there, just don't disturb my projects."

"No problem, Rudy, I'll be sure to leave your projects alone. I'm just here to make some money so I can get my life back on track. You have a good day," Liz answered.

"I should be back before Lenny brings that new model in, but if I'm late, have him wait for me."

"Okay, Rudy."

When Rudy left, Liz looked around. She was surprised that the only surveillance camera the place had was in the front office. She was still going to have to be careful. In case there was also one in the back room.

Liz waited half an hour to be sure that Rudy wouldn't double back, then she locked the front door and made her way to the back room. There was a buzzer on the front door and a camera that showed most of the front office. But with the restroom being in the back, she could always say that's where she was if Radovich caught her in the back.

The back room was actually laid out much nicer than Liz expected it would be. There was a love-seat type of lounge, covered with what appeared to be white lamb skin throws. The lighting was typical for photographic studios she had seen before. Even the restroom was clean and nicely decorated. Some hairbrushes and makeup were on the counter. And she didn't see any sign of a camera.

From inside the bathroom, Liz called Steve at work who seemed surprised to hear from her. "I didn't expect to hear from you so quickly. What's up? Get fired already? Just hoping."

"Wise ass!" Liz quipped right back. "But I do have a question," she said to Steve in a low whisper. "I want to start snooping, the owner told me about the surveillance camera in the front office. I just don't know if there might be cameras or other security stuff that might betray me. Know anybody you can ask?"

"We have a security guru at the shipyard," Steve said. "Let me ask him and I'll call you back."

"Better just text me from now on, until I tell you I've left at the end of each day. I don't want Radovich to get suspicious. I'll also just have my phone on vibrate. If I don't call you right back, that's because I'm not alone."

About fifteen minutes later, Steve texted Liz and she called him back. Steve said, "Ralph was curious about why you were trying to get around surveillance and security, but I reminded him that you worked for the DA, and you are doing research. That satisfied him. He said that a small business can afford several cameras, but they would all be linked to one main recorder. If you can find the recorder, it will probably be digital, with a circuit for each camera. Push the numbered buttons and the current picture from that camera will show up. He said there would also be a video cable in the back, one leading to each camera. But he said that one camera may be focused on the recorder location itself."

"Oh, thank you, thank so much Ste---"

"So, this is me talking now," Steve said, cutting her off. "I don't like what you're doing, Liz. You are treading inside the lion's den here. You're not a security expert. Don't screw up."

"Anything else?" Liz asked.

"I have barely started on the other things he told me. This gets scary, Liz. He said that if you don't find the recorder device, then look for obvious cameras, usually mounted in corners, near the ceiling. He didn't think that a small place could afford sophisticated, miniature cameras, but feel along the top edges of picture frames, top of door jams, and other places that might conceal a small camera. Those are places that may also conceal microphones and small motion detectors. But again, he said that most small places cannot afford any motion detectors smaller than what we'd see in the average home system. He said that if there is a front door buzzer, look at that device because the owner would not have spent money on anything fancier or smaller than that. And oh yes, if you find a camera, try to block its view with something, or if possible, place tape on the lens."

"Wow, Steve. We owe that guy a dinner when this is all over."

"I agree, that's if you're alive and in good enough shape to attend that dinner," Steve said, with more than a little cynicism in his tone.

"Don't be so melodramatic, lover. I'll be fine. I'll call you tonight. And thank Ralph for me." But after all of this information, Liz was a little worried. She hoped she could find anything Radovich may have for security.

Liz did a good search of the back room for cameras. She found none, but she also found no recorder, so she wasn't sure. There was a device on the back door, leading to the alley, but Liz thought it was just another buzzer like the one on the front door. The Dark Room and another room were locked, and Liz felt that maybe Radovich didn't see the need for more surveillance. He seemed to work alone, after all.

In the back of the studio, Liz found several 4-drawer file cabinets behind a small desk. Most of the drawers were locked, but one of the bottom drawers on one of the cabinets hadn't been pushed fully closed, so she was able to open it. The files had project names, then with a dash, a girl's first name was listed after it. Liz was about to open a file that was marked, "The Park – Felicity," when she heard the front door buzzer. She quickly put the folder back in the drawer, careful not to fully close the drawer, and quickly went out to the front office.

Out front, Liz found Lenny and a young girl. Liz greeted him. "You're Lenny, right? If you remember, I was here yesterday with Mr. Radovich when you came in. My name is Liz. I'm working with Mr. Radovich, taking care of the shop. I thought you were coming later?"

"I forgot that we only had a half-day of school today. Linda lives on the other side of town, so once she goes home, it would be a long way for her to come back this afternoon. Will Mr. Radovich be back soon?"

"He may not get back until around two this afternoon. I think he was expecting you to come around three when school let out."

"Darn," Lenny said. "We can't wait that long. Linda has to get home soon. Her mom is expecting her."

"Well then, why don't I get some information from Linda, and snap a picture with my phone? I'll tell Mr. Radovich when he gets back."

"I guess that's alright. I was just going to leave Linda here if that's okay. I have to meet someone else in a few minutes. Tell Mr. Radovich he can tell me what he thinks."

"That's great, Lenny. I'm sure that Linda and I can take care of this ourselves."

When Lenny left, Liz brought Linda into the back room. Linda looked a little flustered, but not as afraid as Liz would have expected, coming to an unknown place like this. They sat on opposite ends of the loveseat, and Linda was looking at the lights and nice furniture.

"So, Linda, how old are you?" Liz asked.

"I'll be fourteen next month," Linda replied. "But Lenny thinks I look old for my age, and I could make some good money as a model."

"How do you know Lenny?" Liz continued.

"We go to the same school, but Lenny is older. He's in ninth grade and I'm in sixth. I got held back a year because I missed some school when we moved."

"You live with your mom and dad?" Liz asked.

"Just my mom. My dad stayed in Ohio when they divorced."

"I suppose your mom works? What does she do?"

"She works days at Wal-Mart and has a part-time job at the Cracker Barrel at night, out near the highway."

"You must spend a lot of time at home then, on your own?"

"Yeah, but that's okay. I spend a lot of time with my friends. I had a little brother, but he died a few years ago."

"Oh, my! How did he die?"

"He crawled out of his crib and fell down the stairs one night. My mom and I didn't hear him, and we found him at the bottom of the stairs the next morning."

"Oh, that's terrible. Your mom must have felt terrible. Is she okay now?"

"She's better now, but I think she may be drinking too much when she feels sad, you know? I hear her crying sometimes."

"And why do you want this modeling job, Linda? Do you know what you will need to do?"

"I think my mom needs more money, but I don't want her to work more jobs. She's so tired, she sleeps all the time on her days off. I figure if I can make some money, she can be home more. Lenny told me that Mr. Radovich will have me wear costumes and take my picture. If he likes me, he will have me visit some other people who will want to take my pictures."

"Is your mom okay with you being a model, Linda?"

"I'm not going to tell her. I figure that I can just buy things we need, like clothes for me, so my mom won't have to spend her money. If I don't need her to spend money on me, then she won't have to work so much."

"That's really nice of you, Linda. But aren't you afraid of going to see strangers, so they can take your picture?"

"Oh, no! Lenny says that Mr. Radovich only works with nice people. Why would I be afraid?"

"Okay, Linda. Can I get your address and phone number? And I'll snap a couple pictures. By the way, what is the name of the diner where your mom works? What's her name? If I go out there to eat, I'll be sure to give her a big tip."

"Here. Let me write it all down. But you won't tell my mom about this job, will you?"

"No, I won't. And I'll call you to tell you what Mr. Radovich says."

"Thank you, Liz. I like you. And you are really pretty, by the way. Lenny said you were really hot!"

Liz thought that Lenny telling his friends that she was 'hot' said a lot about him. How he became a talent scout for Rudy Radovich was what she hoped to find out, and soon.

When Linda left, Liz couldn't stop thinking about her. Liz knew that Linda was Rudy's type. Very pretty for a 13-year-old and starting to show some femininity, these were the things that seemed to attract 'clients' like the ones Rudy was pimping for. By the time Linda was led down the path, from a few 'innocent' nude shots to sex, she would have either decided to continue or one of Rudy's partners would just abduct her like they did the other 13-year-old whose parents decided not to file charges. Linda may never get a chance to escape and would never be seen again.

Liz didn't want to get caught looking through Radovich's files, so she spent only a few minutes back inside that open drawer. Each of the files had pictures of girls, a few as young as Linda, while others appeared to be in their early twenties. All of the pictures had the girls in loose-fitting costumes. Some of the pictures appeared normal, so he could show them to the girls after he developed them. But Radovich also posed them in plunging necklines that left their breasts exposed, or with open sides. He also had a lot of shots with the girls bent over, their backsides exposed in very tight, short shorts. Liz figured these were the pictures he showed to his potential clients.

Liz looked through four files in detail. In those files, she noted that the format of the pictures was always the same, with many using the same revealing costumes.

As Liz closed the drawer, she saw a small slip of paper laying against the wall, which had fallen out when she opened the drawer. Examining the paper closely, Liz could see that it had been wedged in the drawer in such a way that it would fall out when the drawer was opened. This appeared to be Radovich's 'old-school' method to detect whether Liz was snooping while he was gone. He was depending on simple tactics, rather than technology. She replaced the paper at the edge of the drawer before closing it as she found it.

Liz was up front, flipping through the pages of a magazine when Radovich came back to the shop before two o'clock.

"So, Liz. How was your first day? Any messages?" Radovich asked Liz.

"Just a few phone calls asking for rates, you know people wanting to take pictures for their husbands and girlfriends. You gave me a copy of your rates this morning, so I gave them that information."

Mr. Radovich simply nodded, then added. "I'll let you leave early today. I want to be ready when Lenny comes."

"Oh yes, that's the other thing. Lenny already came by with the girl. They got here around eleven-thirty."

"Oh?"

Mr. Radovich rubbed his chin and looked at Liz, confused. "He said they only had a half-day of school today and he forgot about it when he was here yesterday. He didn't want to come back later because the girl needed to get home."

That seemed to clear things up because the confusion instantly left Rodovich's face. "Damn it. I really needed a new model for a client. Did it look like she would make a good model?"

"Just what's your criteria, Rudy? She looked quite young."

"Pretty face, curves, perky breasts, nice butt? You know? The kind of things a guy wants to photograph."

"I think she's cute but flat-chested, and really no butt to speak of. She's a grade-schooler, Rudy. What do you expect?"

Mr. Radovich looked intensely at Liz, as if deep in thought. "I guess I'll have to talk Tiffany into taking this one," he finally said. "She's lost her spark though. Nice body, but she looks depressed all the time."

"Maybe she's lost her interest in modeling," Liz said. "How old is Tiffany?"

"She's almost sixteen and has been with me for about a year. She was great for a while, but I think she had a couple tough assignments. I was hoping this new girl could replace her. Maybe not."

"My guess would be no, based upon the criteria you just gave me. Does your client only want to shoot pictures of young girls? Maybe I could fill in for this one. How much does it pay?"

"Now, that's an idea. Would you mind? I'd really appreciate it. Can I snap a few shots of you, so I can send him some samples? Then I'll let you know. I usually pay the girls $100, but with your experience, how about $200? But you have to treat my client right."

"How about $250, Rudy? I have a lot of things I need for my new place. I'm sure you're getting a lot more from your client, so you can share a little more."

"Sure. Why not? It's a deal. So, let's go shoot a few samples for Nick. I think he'll like you. I'll give you an extra $20 today for this short photo shoot. That'll make $60 for today. Okay?"

Liz thought Rudy accepted her $250 counter very quickly, so it was obvious that his client was expecting a lot more than just a few pictures.

Radovich directed Liz into the back room and unlocked his costume room. He looked through the racks and picked out a frilly top with both sides fully open. The front of the top had a single button just above the navel. The matching shorts were a few sizes too small.

"These are tight," Liz said as she struggled to get into the shorts.

Mr. Radovich simply looked at Liz and grinned. "They'll show off one of your best attributes."

Liz was somehow able to fit into the shorts, but the top was so loose that everything showed. She then stood in front of the camera and let Mr. Radovich take several shots of her. They all looked like normal pictures until he threw a beanbag on the floor and said, "do you mind bending over to pick that up? You do have a nice-looking posterior, you know."

Liz was flustered. However, she wanted to know the ins and outs of this guy's operation, so she was glad to be front and center of how things worked at this "modeling agency."

When they were done with those shots, Radovich looked content. "These will be great, Liz," he said. "I'll develop these tonight and show them to you in the morning. I bet Nick will look forward to seeing you in person after he sees these. So, here is your $40 for today, and another $20 for letting me shoot these pictures. I'll find a nice costume for you to wear on Friday night. I'm sure that Nick will want a photo session with you."

"Thanks, Rudy. I'll see you at ten again tomorrow?"

"Make it eleven-thirty, Liz. I have a few phone calls to make in the morning."

"Okay. See you then. Thanks for letting me do this customer session. That money will come in very handy."

Radovich watched Liz leave. *"I've finally found an experienced girl that won't freak out with my clients when they want to fool around. I sure can't sell her as a virgin, though. I may need to move those foreign girls into that business pretty soon,* he thought, grinning.

Liz was excited to be getting all this information. But it also made her feel a little scared knowing as much as she was beginning to find out about Rudy and his operation. She had talked herself into what she thought was at the very least a porn photo shoot, and now she had to psych herself into what could be a set-up as a prostitute for the evening. She wondered if she could get enough information by Friday to call in the D.A. for him to set up a bust. And if not, how was she going to handle Nick if there wasn't an arrest that night?

Liz knew she needed to talk to Steve, but she didn't dare tell him everything about the rough spot she had talked herself into. She also knew that she had to do something about Linda, the 13-year-old girl who could have been the one going to see this Nick guy on Friday.

Steve got home from his job at the shipyard a little after four each afternoon. So, Liz called his cell phone while he was driving home and said, "Pull over. I don't want you on the phone while you're driving."

"Wow, are you ever bossy today? I'm on my hands-free, so go ahead."

"Wanna take me to dinner tonight? That fancy Cracker Barrel out on the interstate?"

"Why are we going gourmet? There's a Wendy's around the corner from our apartment."

"I want to meet a lady that works there. And to be honest, I miss you. And oh yes, I need some advice."

"Why do I think the advice trumps missing me on this occasion?"

"If you're nice, and quit giving me a hard time, I also might need some snuggles after dinner, before you drop me back at my rooming house."

"Well, I'm sold. Dinner for snuggles? It'll work every time."

Steve was a Naval Architect and worked at the shipyard in Erie, Pennsylvania. He had started working there after they both finished their degrees at the University of Michigan. Liz asked Steve not to get a job in a large shipbuilding city like Norfolk or Seattle, but Erie? She had thought it might be a nice, midwestern town like Sturgeon Bay. But Erie? Well, she passed the Pennsylvania bar and the District Attorney's office was happy when she applied for the job. But Erie?

Erie was suffering from the '*Rust Belt*' syndrome. Many of the large industrial factories were closed, unemployment was high, and kids from single-parent homes were left alone while their mothers worked several jobs. Teens wanted money for cell phones, video games, clothes, and eventually, maybe for booze and drugs. Liz saw the problems Linda was having. The need for money had made her look for a job, but she wouldn't know where that job was leading her until it was too late. It might destroy her life, like the other 13-year-old whose parents were working with the D.A. Maybe the girl would just decide that prostitution was one of the inevitable parts of life. Liz knew that she couldn't save everyone who was confronted with those decisions, but now, she knew she at least needed to help Linda.

"Can you pick me up at our favorite restaurant, Valerio's?" Liz asked. "I'll be out front, but it's far enough away from my rooming house that my new boss won't see you pick me up."

"I'm hoping you'll explain all the cloak and dagger stuff when I see you."

"If you promise to be nice, I'll explain. This is real casual, so come as you are. Maybe thirty minutes? Okay?"

"I missed you last night, so, I'm on my way. Looking forward to that trucker's food," Steve laughed.

5

Liz - Meddling

Liz was already waiting in the parking lot at Valerio when Steve showed up ten minutes early. "So, does this mean we both missed one another last night?" Liz asked. "And can we wait until the Cracker Barrel parking lot for a nice, passionate greeting? In case one of the regulars here should see us, they might wonder why we're steaming up the windows."

"What's the occasion?" Steve asked. "I was afraid I might not see you until you had this case cracked wide open. You said something about needing advice. Is that because you think my mind works like a criminal?"

"Smart ass!" Liz said, chuckling. "I appreciate your mind for other reasons, although I guess I've exposed you to too many criminal ways in the past. Your mother may never forgive me for that. But tonight, I want us to have an extended dinner. I'm going to ask that Valorie Tanner be our waitress. I met her daughter today. I fear she's being led into a one-way tunnel toward porn and possibly prostitution. She hasn't even turned fourteen yet, and she is so naïve, she doesn't see it coming."

"What are we going to say to Mrs. Tanner?" Steve asked.

"I need to lead into the conversation carefully. If Mrs. Tanner tells her daughter that I've spoken to her, it will blow my cover at this modeling agency. But if I can find a way for her daughter to get a real job, and stay away from this one, that would be great. Linda is just trying to supplement her mom's income, and if she finds out I squashed the job for her, she'll go ballistic."

"Just how do you get yourself into these situations, Miss Trent?"

"Pure talent, Mr. Steiner. Aren't you impressed?"

"Isn't this meddling in someone's private life?

"Maybe, but you know me. I can't just ignore it."

Neither Liz nor Steve normally ate at Cracker Barrels, preferring little *Mom & Pop* diners or good ethnic food, but this was an important first meeting with Linda's mother. They walked up to the hostess and asked if Valorie Tanner was working and if they could be seated in her section. The hostess agreed and seated them at a table near the back of the restaurant.

After a short wait, a frail-looking waitress with her dark brown hair pulled into a loose bun came to their table. Liz guessed her to be in her mid-thirties. She had a sincere smile on her face when she greeted them and introduced herself to them as their waitress for the night.

To Liz, Valerie seemed like a very upbeat person for

someone who had already put in a full day at Wal-Mart, if Linda's information was correct.

Liz ordered an iced tea, non-sweet. "What about you, Steve?" Liz asked Steve after ordering her drink.

"You know? I'm a Michigander, and I've never tried that southern, sweet tea. Let me try a glass. I'm in the mood to experiment tonight."

"Well, sweet tea doesn't exactly sound wild and crazy, but to each his own, right?" Valerie said very light-heartedly.

Valerie came back with the tea and asked Liz and Steve if they were ready to order. They weren't, so they asked Valerie to take care of her other customers and come back when she had time. They were in no hurry.

When Valerie left, Liz said to Steve, "Well, it seems to me that Linda's mom is a pretty normal person. She looks like the type of mom who would be concerned about her daughter. I was afraid she might look like she would be burdened by having kids. This initial image seems to match her daughter's concern for Valerie having to work extra jobs, just to make ends meet."

"What do you plan to do now, Liz?"

"I'm going to trust my gut. Valerie seems like she will be concerned about her daughter, so I'll ask if we can meet her after her shift. Let's see what happens then. I have a good feeling about it."

Valerie came back five minutes later with some more iced tea, "And what's the verdict on the sweet tea? It's usually a love-it-or-hate-it type of thing," she asked.

"I did enjoy it," Steve said, "but I'll switch to the unsweet for my dinner. It's too sweet to be refreshing, in my opinion."

Liz said, "I'm originally from Kentucky, so I made that decision a long time ago. I wondered what Steve would think."

"Are you ready to order?" Valerie asked. "No rush, though. It's a slow night."

"I guess we can order, but we may take our time. Can I ask, are you an Erie native? You have just a touch of an accent, but I can't place it."

"Well, I'm originally from Dayton, but I spent enough time in Tennessee when I was married, that maybe I picked up a bit of their twang."

"That's probably what I'm hearing, a bit of Tennessee, but southern Ohio also has that twang. I'll probably never lose my Kentucky accent. What would you recommend for dinner? We don't usually eat at Cracker Barrel. Actually, I never have. What about you, Steve?"

"Me neither, but I do like catfish. Is their cat pretty good?" Steve asked.

"I'm not a big catfish lover, so I may not be the best one to ask. But we sell a lot of it to the truck drivers if that helps your decision?"

"I'll try it. What are you thinking, Liz?"

"My eyes were on that chicken and dumplings. What do you hear about that one, Valerie?"

"Now you're in my league. That's one of my favorites here. So, you want to try that one, Liz?"

"I think we've settled on it, and I'll take a refill of tea."

"The cat comes with fries and hush puppies, Steve. Is that okay?"

"Sounds great," Steve said. "And I'll switch to the non-sweet as well."

After Liz and Steve had finished eating, Valerie came to clear the table. "Are you just traveling through?" she asked Liz and Steve. "What made you stop at a Cracker Barrel if you've never experienced one before?"

"Can I be honest with you, Valerie?" Liz responded. "And please don't be shocked. We came here to meet you. I hope you don't feel threatened because my intention is just the opposite. But earlier today, I met your daughter, Linda."

Valerie stopped cleaning the table and looked down at Liz with concern.

"Is Linda in trouble? Is she skipping school? What did she do?"

"Nothing like that, Valerie. It's more the opposite. I met her and thought she was a sweet, wonderful girl. She spoke highly of you, and all of the hours you work to support the two of you."

"Then why did you want to meet me? This sounds a little weird, you realize."

"I don't want to talk about it here, while you're working. Can we meet outside after you get done with your shift?"

"My boss actually asked if I wanted to leave early because it's such a slow night. You have me a little worried now, so let me finish the last two tables and be outside in about fifteen minutes. Can you wait?"

"We sure can. I see some nice rocking chairs out front,

and we'll be there. Take your time. And don't worry. This is a good thing."

Liz and Steve paid for their tab and were waiting out front when Valerie came out. She looked very stressed, and Liz was sorry to have upset her. Although she seemed to be upbeat in her conversation, Liz could see that the stress of being a single mother and working two jobs was taking its toll on her. She was much too thin for her size, and she dressed simply. To Liz, it looked like Valerie was also trimming her own hair. Money was obviously tight.

"Okay, so what's going on with Linda? You have me very worried, even though you told me not to be."

"I'm sorry I did that to you, but I needed to take you into my confidence, and I didn't know of any other way. I first wanted to meet you, so I could try to see what kind of person you are. Linda spoke highly of you and was worried about you working too many hours. First of all, can I please ask you not to tell Linda about our meeting with you? I promised Linda that I wouldn't talk to you about this, although I did tell her I might stop at the Cracker Barrel to meet you."

"If there's a good reason to give you my word, I guess I can do that. But first I think I need to hear what's going on."

"That's fair," Liz said. "Once you hear my story, I think you'll understand. I'm new in town and was looking for a job. I started working in the front office at Majestic Modeling. This morning, I guess because school was only a half-day, Linda came into Majestic with a boy, named Lenny. Do you know him?"

"I've heard Linda talk about Lenny, but I've never met

him. I think he's a couple of years ahead of Linda in school, which I don't like."

"That's what I thought as well. And Lenny is working with Majestic's owner to find girls for his modeling business. Linda wants to start modeling, so she can make money to help you. She told me that if she could buy her own clothes and things, you wouldn't have to work so many hours."

"She's a real sweety," Valerie said. "I had no idea she was worried about me."

"But Linda hasn't asked you about modeling, has she?"

"No. This is the first I've heard about it. And I'd want to know more about the job before I'd let her do this."

"That's why I'm here, Valerie. I don't think that Majestic Modeling is the best place for Linda to work. I'm working there just for some quick money, but I think Majestic's clients are not all the type that Linda should be around. If we can help Linda find a better job, it would be for the best. Do you understand?"

"Am I hearing that this modeling business might lead to something unsavory, Liz?"

"I can't say that for certain, but I'd feel guilty if I didn't warn you now that I don't think it's the best for your daughter. The problem is that Linda will be very upset if we take away the chance for her to earn some money. She wants to help you. That was the reason she came to the agency with Lenny. And by the way, I don't think Lenny has Linda's best interests in mind. He's just looking for a finder's fee from Majestic. Tell me a little about yourself. Have you been to school? Could you find a better job, with fewer hours?"

"I started college years before," Valerie began, "but I met this guy from Tennessee and fell for him and ended up pregnant with Linda. He married me, but he wasn't really in love with me. We divorced when he started running around with a couple of barflies. I came out of the divorce pregnant with another child, so I had a four-year-old and a baby. My parents tried to help so that I could stay in college, but my dad died from lung cancer, and I had to leave school. I had about a year left for my degree. I was living near my mom in Ohio, and my baby boy died in an accident before he turned two. It took me a while to get over that, and not sure if I am yet, but Linda was old enough to suffer the loss as well."

"That's terrible, Valerie. It had to have been tough to survive that. But I could tell that Linda respects you and worries about you. So, what brought you to Erie?"

"I would have fallen apart if it wasn't for Linda. I knew I needed to survive for her. It was tough, but I'm still here and tryin'. We moved to Erie about six months ago because of the college here. I wanted to finish my degree. I just haven't had the income to go back to school yet, so I'm sorta' drifting right now."

"What degree are you trying to finish, Valerie?"

"It was called Legal Aid, or Legal Assistant, back in Ohio. I was hoping to become a Paralegal like my mom had been when she was younger."

Liz wanted so much to tell Valerie about her connection to the District Attorney's office, but the timing was all wrong. Instead, she told Valerie that Steve worked at the shipyard and could ask the managers there if they knew of a way to get her back in school. "But for right now, what do we do about Linda's wanting a job? I wonder if there might be something safer for her to be doing. Maybe there are better modeling agencies around, that would involve a parent to be sure the child is protected," Liz added.

The three of them sat in silence for some time. Valerie was the first to speak. "Liz, do you realize how shocked I am right now? You don't know me at all, and you just met my daughter today. Most people would have ignored the warnings you saw, and Linda might be mixed up in something terrible. Why are you even concerned?"

Steve was the one to answer, "If you knew everything about Liz that I do, you wouldn't be surprised. She takes the welfare of people she meets as her responsibility. It does drive me nuts sometimes, but I guess that's why I love her."

"Quit it, Steve. You'll make me start crying. But Valerie, maybe you can start a conversation with Linda, ask her if she has thought about trying to make extra money. Have you heard enough to give me your word, not to tell Linda that I spoke to you?"

"Oh, certainly, Liz. I cannot thank you enough for finding me and telling me about all of this. I won't betray your confidence with Linda. But I'll bring up the extra money issue with her, and help her find some part-time job that makes her happy."

"And please keep in touch with us, so that we can help you get back in school this fall. And if we see a possibility for a job that Linda could fit into, we'll also get in touch. But for now, try to keep Linda away from Lenny. I think he could be trouble.

"Steve, would you give Valerie one of your cards? Can she call you at the shipyard if she wants to talk to me? I don't have a cell phone right now."

"Sure thing, Liz." And Steve handed Valerie a business card.

On the drive back to Liz's place, Steve started quizzing Liz on how she was going to work on Valerie's problems with college, find Linda a job at thirteen, and still keep herself safe. Liz admitted that she had bitten off a few tough projects again and that she wasn't quite sure how to proceed.

"I know some of the guys at the shipyard are Gannon University grads. I'll ask them tomorrow whether any degrees at Gannon could help Valerie become a Paralegal. I assume you were thinking she could work in the D.A.'s office?"

"Yes. I didn't expect that would be her goal. But wouldn't that be great?"

"And what about the little girl? Even store shelf stockers need to be 16 years old. That's going to be tough."

"I'll need to think about that one. But seeing that we spent all of my hug-time talking to Valerie, I think you need to drop me at my rooming house. Maybe we can catch up on hugs later in the week."

"Maybe Friday we can catch dinner, and you can spend the night at our apartment? I'm missing having you around, you know."

"My goodness, this is only the second night. Just what are you saying?" Liz said with a smirky grin on her face. "But I have something I need to do on Friday. Sorry, my man. Maybe Saturday?"

"I think I've gotten used to us being a real couple these last few months. I hope this undercover stuff isn't going to last very long. Is Friday something to do with this project?"

"Yes. I'm hoping that Friday could get me the evidence we need."

"Is it safe? What you're doing on Friday, I mean?"

"Of course, it's safe," Liz lied.

"By the way, what about the surveillance questions you asked me to find out about? Did you find any cameras or other things in his studio?"

"Nothing that sophisticated. However, I did find some 'tells' as the Kentucky Troopers used to call them. The amateurs, and even some tricky perps, plant little pieces of paper in drawers, which fall out when the drawer is opened. I found one in a partially opened file drawer today, but I saw it had fallen on the floor. I think he placed it there to test me. Luckily, I saw it and replaced it."

"Well, see? He's not as stupid as you think. Please...be careful. I'm worried about you," Steve said.

"I'm being careful. Don't worry about me, my love!"

"Yeah, right!" Steve said, as he kissed Liz and said good night.

Liz asked Steve to drop her off around the corner a block away from her rooming house just in case Radovich happened to be leaving his shop, which was on the same street. When Liz walked into the dining room, she found Ruth Behrendt vacuuming the carpet. "What are you doing working this late,

Ruth? I know you make breakfast for most of your tenants. You should be sleeping by now."

"Can't afford a cleaning lady, so I need to do it all myself. I'm used to hard work. Don't worry."

"Maybe you could find someone to help you part-time, Ruth."

"If I could find someone, sure. But where? I can't pay a lot."

"I met a young girl today, looking for part-time work. I could have her mother call you. They live just a few blocks away."

"I'd consider it. Thanks, Liz. Have the girl's mother call me. I certainly would like some help."

"The girl is only fourteen," Liz kinda lied, "but I think she's a serious young lady. She wants to earn a little money to help her mother."

"It might be a good match. I hope it works out. Have her call."

Liz thought, *thank you, God! You were listening!*

6

Looking Sleazy

The next morning, Liz arrived at Majestic at about eleven-fifteen. She heard Radovich working in the back room and headed quickly back there. She was hoping not to give him time to put everything away. "You sure are a prompt little vixen," Rudy said when Liz walked in. "I told you that you could come in later today."

"I'm only fifteen minutes early. So, what's the plan for today?"

"First, let me show you the pictures I shot with you last night. I think you'll like them. I sent some to my artist customer, and he'd like to meet you on Friday."

Liz had seen some of his previous work on some of the other young girls, but she was still surprised by how professional the photographs looked. Not what she had expected at all. However, she did not see any of the more candid shots that Rudy had taken, like bending over to pick up the bean bag, and other more revealing shots she knew he'd taken when she wasn't looking. She heard the camera lens when she was adjusting her loose-fitting top. "They look very nice, Rudy. You're a good photographer. If you have somewhere to go, I can straighten up the back room for you."

"No, please leave everything right where it is. I know just where everything needs to go, so I'd get confused if you tried to help. Just leave it all alone, please."

"Okay, Rudy. I understand. I'll just stay up front unless I need to use the restroom. You can head to your appointments. I know you're a busy man."

Liz could see the worried look on Radovich's face, but she could also tell that he didn't want to rush around, putting things away, which might look to Liz like he was trying to hide things.

"Will you be back by six o'clock? I could stay longer if you needed me to stay."

"I should be back by then, but you can leave at six if I'm running late. Just lock the door and pull it shut."

"Okay then, Rudy. You have a nice day."

"Thank you, Liz." And he left.

Again, Liz waited for a half-hour to be sure that Radovich didn't come back. Liz figured that Radovich either trusted her, or thought she was stupid, because at least half of the drawers in his file cabinets were partially open, and Liz also found the door to his dark room unlocked. That door had been locked the day before, so she figured that was a good place to start.

When Liz opened the Dark Room, her peripheral vision barely caught the view of something fluttering to the floor, behind the door. She looked at it and realized that Radovich had planted a small piece of clear cellophane on top of the door. The wrapper looked like it had come from some sort of candy wrapper. Liz set the cellophane aside. It was now obvious that Radovich had not reached a full level of trust with her. She now knew for certain that he was watching her, and she needed to be careful and observant. At least, it seemed, since he was using such cheap and unconventional security tricks, that he did not have any hi-tech security. She could find her way around cellophane and candy wrappers, but hidden security cameras would have been trickier for sure.

Liz went about her business, careful not to disturb the position of anything she looked at. The first things she saw were a couple of photos of herself on the drying rack, in the very unflattering positions he had caught in his candid shots. He had zoomed in on the images and printed close-ups of any areas where her breasts were partially exposed. The zooming into her backside upset her. She had known what he was doing, but seeing the actual prints, was shocking. It showed details she would be embarrassed for even Steve to see. Liz started snapping photos with her cell phone but realized that Radovich was smart enough not to have Liz's face in the shots where her body parts were exposed. Not very good evidence!

When Liz came back out to the desk area, she replaced the cellophane on top of the Dark Room door. Liz was surprised that Rudy didn't employ more security around the studio, but realizing that he had come from Bosnia, she figured he was more used to employing these simple signs. If she hadn't noticed them on the drawers the previous day, she might not have noticed. She was just about to walk away when she noticed that a desk drawer was partially open. She pulled it open all the way, watching for any paper, cellophane, or other of Radovich's 'tells'. Inside, she found a portable hard drive lying on top of some other unorganized files. Liz picked up the drive and studied it briefly, watching for anything to fall free. *What if it contains all of the raw data for Radovich's photos,* Liz thought to herself. She knew it couldn't hurt to find out, so she called Steve at work and told him she'd found something and needed his help.

"If this gets you out of this project quicker, I'll be right there," Steve simply said.

"Good, Steve, can you meet me here in a few minutes with a laptop computer? Come around to the alley. I'll let you in through that door," Liz said.

Twenty minutes later, Liz was letting Steve in through the back door. They were both shocked when a buzzer went off. Liz was afraid it was someone at the front door, but when she closed the alley door, the buzzer stopped. She handed Steve the hard drive and showed him where to work at an empty table in the back room.

"Can you copy the contents while I stay out front? I'll watch for Radovich. And by the way, don't move anything. I think he knows just how he leaves things, so I don't want him suspecting that I was snooping around. I'll leave the door to the front office open. When you hear me drop this heavy book, it means Radovich is coming. Get the heck out through the alley door."

"Okay, but this could take a while, depending on how much is on this drive."

"Let's hope we can get it all before he comes back," Liz said, giving Steve a quick kiss before leaving the room and leaving the door open, as planned.

A little over an hour later, Steve walked out of the back room looking for Liz. He was done copying the contents of the drive. He handed it to Liz, and she quickly saw him out the same way she had seen him in. But before he left, Liz asked Steve to check the contents on the drive to see if it was readable. Then she thanked him and promised to call him later.

After Steve left, Liz relocked the back door and went back to Radovich's file cabinets. One cabinet was already open and was marked 'ASIA.' Liz went carefully through the folders looking to memorize how they were organized so that she could leave them just as she had found them. The first file she opened belonged to a young Asian girl. Liz estimated her to be either fifteen or sixteen. The top photo was very flattering, using the same costumes she'd seen in other photos.

As she flipped further into the folder, the photos became more explicit. There were many shots of the girl's genitalia fully exposed. Liz looked through others and opened one marked 'Linny.' By this time, Liz was visibly shaking, she almost dropped the folder. The young girl in the photo could not have been more than seven or eight years old. She was naked. A hand belonging to someone else was caressing her. It was clear even from the picture that this poor girl was not a willing participant in this serious violation of her body. Her tiny fists were clenched and her body was tense, and there was a sad and frightened look in her eyes.

Liz didn't know how to proceed. This guy was recruiting young, local girls for his operation, but obviously, she had uncovered something even more sinister.

In her previous role at the Kentucky State Police, she had taken an FBI Human Trafficking training class that mentioned something about the importation of young Asian girls for sex. The girls in these pictures, however, were hardly more than babies. Liz found the evidence of its existence quite disturbing. Hearing of its existence was one thing, but personally seeing evidence of it, left Liz in quite a bit of shock.

Thinking she had seen enough for the day, Liz closed the file and quickly looked through several other folders, snapping pictures of what she thought could count as evidence of Rudy's operation. It was apparent from the pictures in the other folders that Radovich was importing girls from Asia and Eastern Europe. So where was he keeping these girls? They couldn't possibly survive out there on their own.

The buzzing of Liz's cell phone interrupted Liz's thoughts. It was a text from Steve.

"Call me when you can," it said.

Liz quickly put everything back in its place and looked at the clock. It was six o'clock and Radovich was still not back, so she called his cell phone and told him she was ready to leave. After he promised to pay her the day's wages of $40 the next morning, Liz locked up and left.

Rudy came back to the studio a little after Liz had locked up and left and was pleased to see that Liz had not disturbed anything. All of his ingenious 'tells' were still in place. It looks like he had found someone he could trust. This would be a big help to his business, and he seemed to have an experienced woman that he could market for higher bids. He was hoping that she'd cooperate. He would learn more after Liz spent the night with Nick.

Rudy was finishing up for the night when he noticed that the alley door had been opened at some point during the day. He could tell because the small piece of scotch tape he had placed on the hinge was wrinkled up. He made a note to ask Liz about it in the morning.

"Can you pick me up? I need some advice, Stevie boy," Liz said when Steve answered the phone. She had just left Radovich's studio.

"Sure. And I have to tell you what I found in those files on the drive. I don't understand much of it."

"Maybe I'd better spend the night at our apartment then. We may have a lot to talk about, and I really need some cuddling. I think I've stumbled into a terrible mess here," Liz said, admitting that she was afraid of what else she might find at Majestic Modeling. Steve sensed her anxiety and left quickly to meet her.

"Where should I meet you?" he asked as he headed quickly to his car.

"Our Italian place works, but let's eat at home. I'm not in the mood to be out in public."

"That bad, Babe?"

"Yup. You know I don't shock easily, but I'm now officially in shock."

"Okay, sweetheart. I'm on my way," Steve said. He knew this had to be serious for Liz to admit she was in shock.

7

Asian Imports

Liz was already sitting on the rock ledge in front of Valerio's when Steve pulled into the parking lot. She looked dejected. Liz hopped into the passenger seat when Steve pulled up to her.

"Let's not talk until we get home," she said as soon as she was seated. She didn't utter another word from that point on. Steve had seen this side of Liz before, the time when she had found out that one of the trafficked girls she was looking for, had been killed. The girl's abductors had killed her with an overdose of animal tranquilizers. This was why Steve had hoped Liz would keep her promise and stay away from undercover work. She took these terrible things very personally. He wouldn't expect her to be any other way, but repeatedly exposing herself to these things was seriously affecting Liz's health, and they both knew it.

When they were finally in their apartment, Steve asked Liz if she wanted to go first and reveal what had her looking so dejected, but she simply shook her head and told Steve to go first.

"I think you'd better start," Liz said to Steve. "Once I tell you what I've found, I may become a basket case."

"Well, in that case, I'd better go first," Steve replied. "At first, I thought we didn't have anything worthwhile on that drive, because you said we were expecting photographs. But then I found some PDFs of forms and documents. Most of them were trucking company invoices, so I didn't think anything of them. But then I started seeing frequent payments Radovich was making to some guy in Long Beach. At first, I thought he was buying wine. The invoice said, 'Two (2) 6-year-old, three (3) 8-year-old, one (1) 12-year-old,' and so forth. But one of them said, 'One (1) male, approx. 58, one (1) female, approx. 55,' which I didn't understand."

Liz began to cry, "I think I do. I wondered how he took care of the young ones. He's also buying babysitters."

"You lost me on that one, Liz. What does all of this mean?" Steve was genuinely confused.

"I thought Radovich was just using local girls for porn and prostitution. But today, after you left, I found pictures of young Asian girls, with a few that I thought might have been from Eastern Europe, judging from the costumes he put them in. Many of the photos showed little girls naked and posed in very demeaning ways. He is a much sicker man than I thought. What am I going to do, Steve?"

"You need to call your boss, Liz. And I mean the District Attorney, not Radovich. This is going to get out of control. It's already way beyond what you expected, and if Radovich thinks you're working undercover, your life will be in danger, and you know it. I thought the people you uncovered in Kentucky and Michigan were bad, but I think this guy is much more dangerous."

"I think you're right, Steve. But I can't just back away. We don't know where he's keeping these young ones. I need to stay on the inside until we find them."

"I understand, Liz. But you have to ask for help, and you have to do it now. You can't handle this one alone."

Liz nodded. "Okay. I'll call Mr. Pierson in the morning before I head to the agency. For now, I need some wine and a lot of snuggles. This has been a bad day."

Liz called Tom Pierson at home the following morning. She knew he arrived at his office by eight, so she decided to call him before he left home to go to the office.

When Tom Pierson answered the phone, Liz cut right to the chase. "Mr. Pierson, it's Liz Trent. Can we meet this morning? I think this modeling agency operation is much worse than we suspected. I've uncovered some terrible things, and I don't know how to proceed."

"I was getting worried about you, Liz," Tom replied. "I'm glad you called. I didn't want to blow your cover by calling you. I'll head out to the office now. Can you be there in a half hour?"

"Yes. I'll be there. See you soon, and thanks," Liz answered.

Steve dropped Liz off at the District Attorney's office on his way to work. Before he drove off, Steve asked Liz to promise that she would let the police do the dirty work. "Remember, you aren't a cop anymore."

"Yes, I promise," Liz responded, her fingers crossed behind her back. She knew promising Steve that she would leave it all to the police was not what she really intended to do, but it was what he needed to hear, and so she promised him that she would.

"Please email those shipment invoice documents to my DA-Office address," Liz said to Steve before heading inside. "And thanks, lover."

"Call me and tell me what happens next. I worry about you, Babe."

"I'll call when I can. Don't worry about me."

"When I hear you say that, I really start worrying. I don't trust that part of your life. Please....be careful!"

Tom Pierson was at his desk when Liz walked in. He had brought her an extra strong Americano, knowing she loved her morning wake-up. "Thanks, Mr. Pierson. You remembered."

"If you're still on your Leave of Absence, just call me Tom," he said. "So, what have you found to help our case?"

"Tom, I think... no... now... I know that Radovich is importing young girls from Asia and elsewhere and selling their bodies for sex." Liz pulled out her cell phone and showed him the pictures.

"How do you know they've been imported, Liz?"

"Yesterday, Radovich left his desk open, and I found a portable hard drive in a drawer he usually keeps locked. I had my good man, Steve, come by with his laptop, and we downloaded the hard drive. Steve will be emailing me copies of the documents he found. The documents show that Radovich has been paying someone in Long Beach for imports, those imports appear to be young girls, and maybe some boys. And get this…he's also imported adults. I think the adults care for the young ones. I just don't know where, and that's where I need help."

'That's awful, Liz. I hope we can get to the bottom of this as soon as possible," Tom replied.

"I sure do hope we can, too," Liz said.

"I know you well enough, Liz. I'm sure you have a plan. Give me details when you know more, and I will see how I can help."

"Actually, you might be able to help me now."

"Really? How's that?" Tom asked.

"Radovich seems to trust me already. He leaves me alone to take care of the studio, and I suspect he goes to where those girls are being kept. He meets me at the studio each morning and then leaves. Can we arrange for a good tail to follow him? You know the local police better than I do, so we need someone who knows how to stay undetected."

"I can see your police experience showing here, Liz. I'm impressed by your plan. And just so you know, I love our local cops, but cops always look like cops. Other than you, young lady, I've never met a cop who can't be detected. So, tell me if this idea will meet your need. I think this is important, and I have a guy who is exactly what we need. His office is just a few buildings down the street, and I can justify hiring a private guy to do this. Can you stay long enough to meet him? When does Radovich expect you?"

"I need to be at the studio by ten."

"Then let me call him and get him over here," Tom said.

Liz waited while Pierson dialed his phone and spoke to a man he referred to as Burt. "Burt, thank God you're in early. I have a job for you, it's kinda an emergency. Can you run over? I have someone here you need to meet."

While they waited for Burt to arrive, Liz went to her desk and checked her emails. Steve had sent her samples of the documents. Liz in turn, printed them out for Mr. Pierson. She was walking the printed copies back to Tom's office when Liz spotted an older gentleman walk into the office. The man talked briefly to the receptionist, and the receptionist pointed him in the direction of Tom Pierson's office.

This guy sure doesn't look like an undercover investigator, Liz thought. *Well, I guess that's probably why Tom uses him.*

Liz stood outside Tom Pierson's door and watched Tom shake Burt's hand.

"Come on in, Liz," Tom eventually said to Liz. "This is Burt Snyder. Looks like he fell off the produce truck, right? That's why I love this guy. He's exactly what you need. Please give Burt a quick rundown of what you've found, and if I can get Burt to take this job on such short notice, I'll have him drop you near Majestic. Then, if Radovich leaves like he usually does, Burt can tail him."

"Majestic Modeling?" Burt Snyder said. "Radovich is the shady bastard that runs that place, right? I've heard nothing good about that scumbag."

Liz smiled. "I like this guy already," she said. "At least we're on the same page about Radovich."

Burt shifted in his chair and looked at Liz, eager to hear

what she had for him. Liz gave Burt a quick rundown about the local girls modeling for Radovich, and what she now knew was an international sex-trafficking operation. She needed Burt to find where Radovich was keeping the girls, probably cared for by an older man and woman."

"If that's what he's been doing, I'd love to be part of taking him down, Liz."

Liz handed the printouts of the payments and truckers' invoices to Mr. Pierson, and without any explanation, Tom said, "If Burt can find the location of these girls, we can nail him with these documents. Now we just need to catch him on the local modeling operation."

"I may have that buttoned up by this weekend, Mr. Pierson. I was so concerned about these young, Asian girls, I never covered that part of my story. Can I talk to you about that tonight? I'll call you at home if that's okay?"

"By all means. You aren't doing anything dangerous, are you?"

"You're starting to sound like Steve. Are you two talking behind my back?" Liz smiled.

"You'd better get out of here. I don't want you to be late for your other boss. And Burt, thanks again for dropping everything else for this."

"No problem," Burt said. "I know that when you call, it's always something important. This sounds like it's critical, and I'd never pass on something like this."

Liz and Burt walked out of Tom Pierson's office and to the parking lot together. Once inside Burt's car, he asked Liz some questions. Liz answered him as he drove her from downtown and out to Majestic. Burt was the perfect undercover man: he wore ratty clothes and looked frail and homeless with gray, unkempt hair. But the thing that Liz liked the most was his attention to small details. Burt had seen Radovich before, so he knew what he looked like, but he wanted details about his car, including any unusual noises it made. Burt said, "I prefer to sit around the corner where he can't see me. I leave my window open and listen for him to start the car. I listen for the squeaks, rattles, loud exhaust, and other noises to know when my man is on the move."

"With that in mind, Burt, you can drop me around the corner. I'll walk through the alley to get to the studio."

"I'll find what you need, Liz. Now watch yourself with this guy. He may be treating you alright now, but if he ever suspects your real motives, I think he could kill someone. He's that type. I like you, young lady, and I don't want to see you get hurt."

"So, Burt. You've been talking to my Steve as well? I'll be fine, but thanks for worrying."

8

Tiffany's Story

Nick liked the younger girls because he was afraid of older prostitutes. He was gentle with the younger girls, but he easily talked them into taking off their clothes for his '*artistic*' photos. He did this by showing them nude photos in magazines and telling them they could one day make it into the pages of those magazines, become famous, and make lots of money. He often described to Radovich how he seduced the girls with lewd acts during his photo shoots.

Radovich once sent an older girl to Nick; her name was Tiffany. Tiffany was another one of the many girls Lenny had brought to Radovich. She only came to see Radovich because she considered Lenny to be her friend. She actually had a crush on Lenny. Tiffany's parents were divorced, and she didn't have money to buy nice clothes. She once asked her mom to buy her a cell phone, and her mother responded angrily, telling her to get a job if she wanted those luxuries.

This need to afford basic luxuries, and her belief in Lenny

as a friend, are what brought her to Majestic Modeling. Like all the other girls recruited by Lenny, Tiffany thought she was getting into modeling. So when the photo shoots started involving nude shots, Tiffany was rightfully confused and embarrassed. However, she'd seen the magazines with topless women models. In the magazines the boys passed around at school, some of these models were nude. In her mind, she thought these poses and pictures were a part of the modeling profession, so she had better adapt if she was going to make the money she wanted to make.

Of course, she did not like having to do these poses, and it's not like she didn't try to get out. She had even gone to Lenny a time or two, expressing her discomfort to him. Lenny had been encouraging the first time, assuring her that her poses were normal and that if she hung in there a little longer, she would make some serious money. The second time, he had snapped at her. "They pay you extra for those nude shots, don't they?" he replied angrily. "Yes," Tiffany had said, a little surprised and hurt by Lenny's comeback. "So why are you complaining?"

Tiffany was upset about Lenny's response, but she didn't want to give up the money. She also didn't dare ask for advice from her mother.

It wasn't long before those nude photos turned into something even more sinister as she was passed from older man to older man as they requested Tiffany for their photo shoots. Tiffany didn't object when the men started touching her. The touching made her uncomfortable, but she began to notice that letting them do so came with added benefits in the form of extra tips.

When Tiffany eventually gathered the courage to complain to Lenny, she was surprised by his reaction. She thought he would step in and console her, but instead, he yelled at her. "Just what do you think a call-girl does, Tiffany? You'd better put out when they start asking for it, or else you're washed up!"

Tiffany was too shocked to cry. She finally realized that Lenny saw her as nothing more than just a call girl, and he didn't care for her at all.

By the time she made her way to Nick, she had lost all confidence in herself and no longer trusted the men she was seeing. She had no one to protect her, and so she did whatever she thought was safe; she complied so she could continue making that extra money. Her mom had told her to find a job, and this one was paying much more than any of her friends were earning, plus the tips were great if she let the men touch and massage her.

Nick had a tough time keeping his hands off Tiffany. And Tiffany didn't fight his advances any longer. Touching soon turned into other lewd acts, and an eventual rape. The night Nick raped Tiffany, he rewarded her with a one-hundred-dollar bill and called Radovich to come and get the girl, because Tiffany had begun crying and wouldn't leave. Nick never told Radovich about what had happened. When they arrived back at Majestic Modeling, Radovich paid Tiffany her $150 for the evening and thought nothing about it, though he saw a change in Tiffany's normal upbeat attitude. He then noticed a permanent change in Tiffany after that night. She seemed very depressed.

When Tiffany sought advice from a friend at school, asking if the girl had experienced sex, the girl said, "So, Lenny finally talked you into fooling around?"

Tiffany told the girl she had sex for the first time with an older man, and wanted to know if sex was supposed to be violent.

"What are you telling me, Tiffany? Are you a prostitute?" The girl replied, with a look of revulsion on her face. "My God, what are you doing?"

With nobody to talk to, Tiffany felt betrayed by Lenny and very alone. A few weeks later, Tiffany took her mother's entire bottle of sedatives. Her mother found her the next morning when she didn't wake up to go to school. Nobody understood why she would take her own life, not even Lenny.

9

Caught in the Act

Liz walked into the studio and found Radovich developing some photos in the darkroom. He scrambled to move and hide things when he heard her coming in. Liz pretended not to notice.

"Good morning, Rudy," she said, greeting him cheerfully. It was hard for Liz to be nice to Radovich, but she knew she had to keep up appearances if she wanted to expose him as the evil man he was.

"Do you have any more plans for today?" Liz added.

"Yes, I might be gone all day again. I left money for both yesterday and today over there on the table. Could you stay late again today? I have a busy day planned."

"Sure, Rudy," Liz replied. "No problem at all."

Liz left the darkroom and went to the front office, followed by Rudy. "So, you're ready for tomorrow's photo session?" he asked her. "The customer is looking forward to meeting you."

Liz cringed but didn't dare let it show. "Yes, I'm all set. Just leave the address for me, and I'll call Uber. You said the man's name is Nick?"

"Yes, his name's Nick," Radovich replied.

He seemed to think for a little bit before he continued, "I'll drop you off, Liz. You can take an Uber home. I don't want you to get lost and be late for the appointment. This week it may be a friend of Nick's. A guy named Phil."

Liz had told Tom Pierson that she would call him with the address, but now she had to find another way.

Before Radovich left the studio, he turned to Liz, a hint of suspicion betraying his smiling face.

"Liz, you opened the alley door yesterday."

Liz was caught off guard. She needed to think of something quick.

"I have a camera set up on my desk to take a picture when the door opens," he seemed to say this to warn Liz that he already knew she'd let Steve in through the door.

"Can I trust you, Liz? Why was he here?"

"Oh, no," Liz said, feigning embarrassment. "Please don't be mad when I tell you why he was here."

Rudy looked at her impatiently, and Liz knew her explanation had better be good.

"I met him at a bar the night before last. I can't take a man to my rooming house, and he lives with his mother."

Rudy's expression changed from impatience and suspicion to understanding, a small smile lifting the corner of his lips, so she continued. "We wanted so bad to have sex but had nowhere to go. I invited him here during his lunch hour yesterday."

Rudy looked at Liz. She was just the kind of gal he needed for the job.

"I hope you aren't mad at me."

Rudy laughed. "I think you are going to work out just fine, you little vixen. I'd rather you don't invite strangers into my back room again, but soon, you'll be making enough money to get yourself a nice, private little apartment. That is... if you can make my customers happy."

That was close, Liz thought. It appeared that Rudy was just happy with the thought that Liz had an active libido.

After Radovich left, Liz texted Steve to let him know that she was okay. She also asked if he would call her when he had some free time. Then she peeped out of the front door to see if she could spot Burt. Liz hoped that Burt was going to stay as incognito as he said he would. She was beginning to see that Radovich was not at all stupid; he was taking no chances.

Steve called Liz back almost immediately.

Liz told him about Burt Snyder and their attempt to tail Radovich. She didn't mention that Radovich knew he had come through the alley door.

"Have you heard the news this morning?" Steve asked Liz.

"No. What news?" Liz asked.

"A young girl at the high school was found dead this morning. Drug overdose."

"Heroine? Meth? What else did the news say?" Liz asked, wondering what this had to do with her mentioning Radovich and Burt.

"The news didn't say. In fact, they are not saying much. But one of the guys at the shipyard said his son is in the girl's class. The rumor out among the kids in school is that she took her mom's prescription drugs."

Liz's curiosity pushed her to ask more questions of Steve. "Did they mention her name? Just curious."

"Not that I recall. I could ask."

"Let me know what you find out. I wonder why she did it. Radovich will be out all day, so text me. I wouldn't want you to call if he happens to come back early."

About twenty minutes later, Steve texted Liz back. "Tiffany Edmunds."

Tiffany Edmunds. Liz remembered that Radovich had mentioned calling Tiffany when Liz told him Linda was not well-endowed and didn't meet his criteria. Radovich had said something about the girl being depressed, and that's when Liz had volunteered to take the appointment with his customer, Nick. Could this be the same Tiffany?

Liz hoped that Radovich would leave the filing cabinet drawers open again. She walked to the back room and found the drawers where she had found the pictures of the very young Asian girls, closed, and locked. She looked at the upper drawers and saw that a few of them hadn't closed all the way, so she started scanning the labels. Radovich was obviously not a very organized man, none of the files were in alphabetical order. Liz looked at each label until she came across one near the back of the drawer, which simply read in letters, "SHY MAN – TIFFANY."

Liz pulled out the folder and opened it. Her hands trembled slightly at the thought of what she might find. In the folder, there was a picture of an older girl, probably about sixteen years old. The girl was beautiful with long dark hair and eyes that looked eager yet sad. This girl also had a few more curves than most of the girls Liz had already seen in these folders. The display of pictures was the same; loose-fitting tops and tight shorts, which left little to the imagination. At least there were no nude shots in this file, but there were some candid shots that seemed like they were taken to give the impression that this girl had breasts almost falling out of her top.

Liz snapped a picture of the girl's headshot and texted it to Tom Pierson.

"Are you aware of the teen suicide in the news? Any chance this might be the girl?"

Within a few minutes, Pierson texted back.

"Can you call me?"

Liz called Pierson, who sounded shocked.

"Is she one of the Majestic girls?" Tom asked Liz.

"Yes, she is. "Liz responded. "I assume this is the girl who OD'd?" she asked.

"I need to pass this information on to the police, but I'll tell them you're working there undercover. What else can you tell me?"

"Radovich was going to send a 13-year-old girl to some guy on Friday. When I nixed that girl by finding something wrong with her, Radovich mentioned sending Tiffany, I assume this Tiffany was the same girl Radovich mentioned. He said she looked depressed all the time and was a little hesitant to send her out. That's the job I'm supposed to be going to tomorrow. It's the job I wanted to talk to you about, later tonight."

"I'm getting more than just worried about you, Liz. This

sounds serious. If you go to that appointment tomorrow, I want you wired and to have a transmitter on you. We'll have people outside, ready to come in and arrest this guy."

"If you saw the costumes Radovich uses... let's just say that a wire will be impossible. But a transmitter in my shoe is doable. Also, Radovich won't give me the address ahead of time. He's dropping me at the meeting personally. I'm not sure how to tell you where I am."

"I've got that covered. Burt has been on the phone with me all morning. He thinks you walk on water, but he also thinks you're crazy, putting yourself in danger like you are. If I ask him to continue the tail tomorrow, he'll jump at the chance, knowing it's for your protection."

"I really like him too. Surely not flashy, but sharp as a tack. Is he finding anything yet?"

"Oh, yes. He has the house where the kids are being kept. It's disguised as a daycare and even has a small bus. Radovich and an older Asian man are delivering girls to places with that little bus. Burt has addresses and pictures of each stop they've made. I'm trying to decide when we should shut the operation down. Burt says that each child he sees going into some house is making him physically ill because he knows what is probably happening to them."

"Tom, I'm not sure if we should wait until after my sting tomorrow. What do you think?"

"This is different than common prostitution, Liz. These customers of his are pedophiles. I want to have as many of those people arrested as possible. But tailing him for one more day means those kids are being abused for another day."

"What does Burt think, Tom?"

"Burt said the scene is weird. The children are not being dragged into those homes. He said they walk in, with no real emotion on their faces. They don't look happy, but they don't kick and scream, either. Burt thinks that this is all they've ever known, and they probably think it's normal for them. It sure doesn't help with the sick feeling in my stomach, however. And now this suicide to top it all off. We can never pin her death on Radovich, but we know he probably caused it by the circumstances he put that poor girl in.

"Let's get your Friday night sting set up. We can probably hold that guy who Radovich set you up with, to keep him from contacting Radovich. The more evidence of perversion you can find, the easier and longer we can hold him."

"That's the plan, Tom. I'm going to act as curious as I can to get him to spill as much as I can."

"I'll have the sheriff set you up with the transmitter. Too bad you can't wear a wire."

"Does the sheriff's IT guy have a Bluetooth microphone with enough range to reach a receiver on the street? I could bury one in my hair if I wore it in a bun. That's not my normal hairstyle but ask them if it can be done. Since Radovich is going to drop me at his client's place, if you're sure we can get Burt to follow him, then maybe he can be the one to have the receiver-recorder close enough to record what happens inside?" Liz suggested.

"They seem to miniaturize everything these days, so it's just a question of distance between you and the receiver. I'll ask Burt, he may be more into these things than the sheriff's office."

"I'd better get off the phone, Tom. I want to take photos of as many files as possible. I'm worried that Radovich might destroy them if he thinks he's in trouble. Find out if I can wear a small microphone. I'll need someone to secure it in my hair to catch the conversation."

"I'll call Burt right now. Call me at home tonight so we can finalize the plan," Tom said.

Liz spent the rest of the afternoon photographing as much evidence as she could access. At about four, later that afternoon, Radovich called to tell Liz she could leave early. Before he got off the phone, he wanted to know if Liz could come in a little early on Friday. He wanted to discuss the appointment with her. Nick had eventually canceled, and so they were going to be meeting with another client named Phillip. Phillip wanted an older girl for his photo session. Liz agreed. "Nine o'clock, or do you want to start earlier?" she asked.

"Nine is fine, Liz. Thank you, my dear!"

Liz didn't like the sweet talk Radovich now used with her. The more she learned about him, the more creeped out she became.

Liz called Tom Pierson after she got off the phone with Radovich. She wanted to let him know that Radovich wanted her to come early the next day to discuss Friday night's customer. Can I get that microphone set up tonight? I think it might be good to have tomorrow morning's conversation recorded also."

"I'm sure it's possible. Burt says he has all the equipment

you're asking for. He can get the microphone into your hair and be close enough to receive and record everything. I should have known that Burt would be up on the latest electronics," Tom said.

"Great. Could Burt meet me tonight at Steve's apartment? I'll have Steve pick me up, and Burt can show me what to do."

"I'm sure that Burt will be happy to help. Shall I have him call you, or might it be better to call Steve?"

"Yes, please have him call Steve. I'm going to lock up and get out of here right away."

Liz called Steve at home, right after she left the studio, and asked him to meet her again at Valerio's. Steve agreed, and Liz told him she was planning to spend the night at home.

"I've missed having you here every night," Steve told Liz.

Liz chuckled and told Steve she missed him too. Then she let him know about Burt Snyder and the possibility that he will be calling Steve.

"Give him instructions to find our apartment, please," Liz said.

"He's not a crazy person, is he?"

"No, just the opposite. You're gonna like this guy. And he'll be my protector tomorrow night on that job I told you about."

"So, he's a 300-pound bodyguard?"

"Not exactly. But please don't pre-judge him. He's much smarter than the 300-pound bodyguard guys."

10

Burt Snyder

Burt was already waiting out front when Liz and Steve arrived at their apartment. He was still dressed in his shabby clothes, which made Liz smile. Burt certainly didn't look like the flashy private eye portrayed on television shows.

"Burt, this is my main squeeze, Steve Steiner," Liz said, introducing Steve to Burt. "Steve, meet Burt Snyder."

"Good to meet you, Steve. I'm here to keep your little lady safe in case she hasn't told you. I may look like some defenseless old man, but you don't want to see me when I get upset. Besides, I blend into the woodwork easily, and people tend to ignore me. That works out well when you're doing surveillance."

"I think this woman needs all the protection she can get," Steve said. "She has a bad habit of jumping into situations that might get her killed."

"You can consider me as that annoying uncle. I'm stuck to her like glue from now until this sting operation is over.

Unless I know she's under your care, Steve, I'll be nearby. I sleep, eat, and even have a relief tube in my car. I take my job seriously, and this woman of yours has impressed me. You can trust me to keep her safe."

"Liz has spoken highly about you, so I'm glad you're taking her welfare so seriously. But tell me, how did you get into this line of work?" Steve asked.

"I was in the Marines and had sergeant stripes when we went to the Gulf War. I was wounded and came home for rehab, but the Marines made me take a medical discharge, even though I wanted to stay. I applied to the FBI and was accepted. I went through all their training and was assigned to an office in Youngstown, part of the Pittsburgh District Office. I seemed to have a habit of acting before I was given permission when I saw people in trouble. My methods were not appreciated by my superiors, and rather than be terminated, I decided to resign."

"That almost sounds like Liz. No wonder she likes you," Steve said. "So why Erie?"

"I was originally from a small town, west of here, and there were no serious investigators in the area, so I contacted the local law enforcement agencies, got my license, and set up shop. I only work on divorce cases when I'm hungry. I hate those. The D.A., Sheriff, and even the FBI keep me busy on serious cases where they cannot commit their own people to full-time surveillance. I'm so happy to see Liz working on this sex-trafficking problem. I've seen it going on, but until someone is willing to go to the police and file a complaint, it just gets ignored."

"That is the root issue, Burt," Liz replied. "The parents don't notice until their kids are in over their heads, and then they don't want to put their son or daughter through the trauma and embarrassment of testifying at a jury trial. At best, the local operation ceases for a while until a new trafficking operation moves into town. Because there are always customers wanting sex with young girls, there will always be scum like Radovich to fill their needs."

"Then let's set up tomorrow's sting, so we get the goods on Radovich. I've seen what he's doing with these young Asian girls. We need to stop his entire operation and send him away for as long as possible. You know what happens to traffickers and pedophiles in prison, and I won't feel sorry for him," Burt said.

"Radovich asked me to come in early tomorrow so we can discuss this photo shoot client of his," Liz said. "I hear from Mr. Pierson that you have a small microphone you can hide in my hair, and you can receive the audio in your car. Is that right?

"I have it right here," Burt said, showing the microphone to Liz. It was no larger than a small hearing aid.

"Then, can we start recording tomorrow morning? I'm thinking Radovich may incriminate himself during that conversation. But at least we'll have his instructions to me on tape."

"That's simple. I'll be in the alley before nine, ready to record your conversation."

"The plan for tomorrow evening is for Radovich to drop

me at his customer's place around six. He hasn't given me the address, so I'd like for you to tail us."

"That's also easy," said Burt. "I have a different car for tomorrow just in case he's already spotted the cars I've used to tail him in his daycare bus, and he might recognize it. I can track you and listen to your conversations. The audio may be garbled while I'm tailing you, but I can track you, just like tracking your phone. Then, once Radovich leaves, I can get close enough to your location to record every word. Just try to stay away from music or other background noises."

"Finally, I was going to use a panic button in my shoe to call for help," Liz said. "But I think I can just set up a code signal with you, seeing you'll be listening to me."

"We can do that, but I also have a small transmitter, which can be used as a panic button back-up. It's small enough to place wherever you want, even behind your ear. If I hear the signal from that transmitter, I'll call the Sheriff for back-up, and I'll barge in. I have a battering ram for the door, if necessary. I've already warned the Sherriff that this could happen."

"If this guy doesn't seem to be violent, I'd prefer that you and I take him down. I'll give you my District Attorney's I.D. for me to take when you come in, and we may be able to convince him to cooperate. Are you okay with that, Burt? Do you carry a gun, if needed?"

"I'm permitted, of course. My guns are usually in my trunk, but I'll be armed tomorrow. Try to get his front door unlocked, but I can break in if I hear you're in trouble. I'll have that battering ram ready, just in case."

Steve said, "These conversations scare me, but I feel good, knowing that Burt has your back."

"I told you he's better than a 300-pound bodyguard," Liz said.

Burt said, "Trust me. In these circumstances, brains and technology will always trump brute force."

Then Burt brought out the micro-mini microphone and the mini transmitter, as well as a charger to use overnight. He showed Liz how to attach them, and then he asked Steve to accompany him to his car, so they could test them.

"I'm going to drive away from your apartment until I lose audio communication," he told Liz. "You keep talking, and vary your voice, from mumbling, to normal, and occasionally a scream, like you were in trouble. Give me about five minutes so I can be at least five blocks away, then hit the panic button. I want Steve to see that you'll be safe."

Burt and Steve went out to Burt's car, and Liz started talking, "Burt, don't let Steve feed you any lies about me. I'm really much nicer that Steve will be telling you," And then she screamed, "Help! Steve is a creep." Then Liz continued her quips, hoping that Burt and Steve would be laughing. She timed herself for approximately five minutes, then pushed the small transmitter on the panic button. A few minutes later, Burt's car came back to the apartment.

Burt came in and said, "Didn't you talk? We never heard a thing." Liz looked worried.

Then Steve said, "And I am not a creep!" Then Liz slugged Steve pretty hard on his bicep, causing Steve to wince.

"See, Burt? I told you she was violent. See what I have to put up with?"

As Liz wound up to slug Steve again, he backed up with his hands out and started laughing.

Burt said, "I like you two. You're both nuts."

"And did the mic and panic button work?" Liz asked.

"It worked great," Burt said. I could record full audio up to two blocks away, except when we passed another car. There was no interference at one block. We had garbled audio up to four blocks, but I was able to track you right up to the time you pushed the panic button, which was just short of six blocks. Once Radovich leaves tomorrow, I should be able to park on the same block as your location, so we'll have full audio to record."

"Also, Burt, I'll read the house number of the location as I walk up the sidewalk, just to be sure you have the correct address, in case we need the Sheriff's Police."

11

Liz - Photoshoot

On Friday morning, Liz placed the microphone in her hair, and she walked from her rooming house to Majestic Modeling. Radovich was already in the back room when Liz arrived. He was all smiles when he saw her.

"Thanks for being on time, Liz," Radovich said, studying Liz. Liz tried to stay calm but found herself fidgeting with her hands. If Radovich noticed that Liz was nervous, he did not let on. "I have some errands to run today, but I'll be back early, so you can go to your apartment and get prettied-up for Phillip," Radovich continued. "He's a fairly new customer, so I want you to look good for him."

"I will," Liz replied. "Is Phillip another photographer?"

"He is. He takes photos and then makes paintings from what he photographs. I've seen some of his work, and he's quite good."

Liz nodded.

And then, as if it were an afterthought, Radovich added,

"Most of the women he shoots are partially nude. You're okay with doing that, aren't you, Liz?"

"Of course, Rudy."

Rudy nodded, obviously pleased with Liz's response.

On his way out the door, he told Liz he would be back around two, so Liz could go home and get ready for the shoot and return to the studio before six so they could head over to meet Phillip.

Later that afternoon, Radovich returned a little before two o'clock and told Liz to go home, clean up, do her hair 'real nice,' and then come back to Majestic before six o'clock. When she returned, Radovich handed her a bag from a local department store. He said it was a nice costume for her photo session, and she could put it on after she arrived at the customer's place. He then said he'd drive her to her session. On their way out the door, Radovich handed Liz $100, which he said was her $40 for the day, and extra for a taxi to get home that evening.

Radovich reminded Liz that the customer's name was Phillip, and he was an artist who liked to paint pretty girls. He based his paintings on the photos he would take that evening.

After a short drive, they pulled into the driveway of a small townhome. Radovich said he'd wait until Phillip came to the door. Liz got out, said 1239 Winston, so Burt could hear her location, and rang the doorbell. A man with a clean-cut appearance, also a bit nerdy, who appeared to be about forty-five, came to the door. He looked Liz over for a full minute, then she saw him give a quick thumbs-up to Radovich, and Rudy pulled away.

Phillip invited Liz inside and led her up the stairs to the second floor. He appeared nervous when he offered Liz a glass of wine. Liz only agreed to take it because the wine was still sealed when he opened it. Phillip tried to make small talk, and Liz asked him what kind of artist he was.

"I paint in oils. That one above the sofa is one of mine," he said.

Liz turned to look, and as suspected, the painting was of a nude woman. She was reclining on what appeared to be the same sofa Liz was sitting on. The painting wasn't very good, so Liz said, "Wow. That must have taken a lot of time."

Phillip said, "I understand that Rudy sent you here with a nice costume for tonight's photos. Would you like to put it on for me?"

Liz asked where the restroom was so that she could change. She noticed the disappointed look on Phillip's face, and Liz figured he had expected her to change in front of him. He still pointed down the hall.

Liz went into the restroom and opened the bag. This costume was worse than the one she had worn for Radovich's sample photos. There was a thong, a very small miniskirt, and a top that barely covered her nipples. It was pretty obvious that Phillip expected to see everything tonight! Liz mumbled in soft tones, hoping Burt could hear her, "This guy isn't dangerous. I'll see what I can find out."

When Liz walked back into the living room, Phillip smiled. "Rudy said you were a little older, but a real beauty. He sure was right. How old are you?"

"I'll be twenty-one in a month. Do you normally photograph younger girls?"

"Rudy was supposed to have a fourteen-year-old girl this week, but he said she couldn't make it. But you look great. He said your name is Liz?"

"Yes. Liz. So, what kind of pictures do you want?" Liz asked.

"I like pictures to use for my oils, like the one I painted there on the wall."

"Can I see some of the pictures you've taken before, so I'll understand exactly what you want me to do?"

"Sure. Why not? If that will help you get in the mood." Phillip led Liz to his bedroom, where he opened a drawer filled with photos. Liz didn't see any of them that looked professional, and most of the girls were topless, and some were completely nude. It was obvious that most of these girls were young teens, and she thought she saw a much younger picture of Tiffany, the girl who had committed suicide.

"Where do you want to take these pictures, Phillip?"

"Well, I thought we could get to know one another first, and take pictures later."

At that point, Phillip took off his shirt and started to undo his pants, and Liz said, "What are you doing?"

"First, I want to see if your body is worth photographing. I thought you were an experienced model."

"Of course I am, but why are you taking your clothes off?" Liz asked, genuinely perplexed at how fast and easily Phillip was moving.

Phillip paused to look at Liz with raised eyebrows. "Rudy said you've been around, is that not why you're here?"

"No!" Liz said. "I'm here so you can photograph me. Rudy said something about partial nudes, but he did not mention anything about sex."

"Of course. I thought Rudy told you that."

"No, he didn't. He said you were a new customer. Are you saying this was a setup to have sex with me?"

"Well, yes. Sex... and photographs, but why play around when we can just get right to it."

Liz was flustered but tried to stay focused. "I was not aware of sex, but now that you've made it clear exactly what's expected here, I want you to meet someone."

Phillip looked around the room, confused.

"Can you hear me, Burt?" Liz said to no one in particular.

"My name is Phillip. Who is Burt? Rudy always sends me young girls. I thought you'd be different," Phillip said.

Just then, the doorbell rang. Phillip looked surprised, worried even. "What's going on? Who's at the door?" he asked Liz.

"If you don't want Burt smashing your door to splinters, I suggest you answer the door."

Liz followed Phillip down the stairs. When he opened the door, Burt burst in. He handed Liz her I.D., then Liz turned to Phillip, who still looked very confused by what was going on, and told him he had two choices. He could either agree to cooperate with Liz on the investigation into the Majestic Modeling operation, or Liz could call the police and have him arrested for perversion with minors.

"I don't understand," Phillip stammered. "I invited you here for a nice evening and drinks. What are you saying?" Phillip obviously did not fully understand what he was involved with.

"I think we need to talk, Phillip," Liz said to him. "I used to work for the District Attorney, and I'm now privately investigating the Majestic Modeling operation. If you just expected to take pictures tonight, I might not have been very upset, just shocked. But you jumped directly into expecting sex, so we're going to have a serious talk. I want to know everything you know about Majestic Modeling and Rudy Radovich."

"Why should I talk to you?" Phillip said.

"Because if you don't, Burt will just call the Sherriff right now. If you cooperate, I'll do what I can to reduce your charges."

"I don't see what I've done wrong. You said that you were twenty years old," Phillip said, with his voice quivering.

"I could quote you the Federal Statues on Child Exploitation and Obscenity. The pictures you showed me in your bedroom were taken of minors, in various stages of undress. That is a violation of Federal Statutes against the Sexual Exploitation of Children. Specifically, the photos you just showed me are the production of child pornography, which is a felony."

"But Rudy told me that as long as I don't sell them, it's not a problem," Phillip said, almost whining.

"And you wanted to believe a pimp, who was taking your money for sex with children?"

"I was always very gentle. I promised Rudy I would be gentle."

"By the way, do you know a guy named Nick? He's also a customer of Majestic, right?" Liz asked.

"Nick is my business partner. He told me to call Rudy," Phillip answered.

"How much did you pay Radovich for these evening sessions?" Liz asked.

"I think I'd better stop talking. I need a lawyer," Phillip said.

Liz asked Burt to call Mr. Pierson and tell him they needed a warrant to search Phillip's home. Pierson was friends with the judge who typically handled child abuse cases, and he had already called the judge at home, expecting the need for a warrant. As soon as the judge heard it involved child pornography, he agreed to sign a warrant to search Phillip's premises and to hold Phillip overnight for questioning.

Burt and Liz sat with Phillip and waited for the warrant to arrive. When the sheriff's deputy finally arrived, Liz showed the warrant to Phillip before legally reentering the premises. Liz led the investigator into the bedroom and pointed to the drawer containing the photos Phillip had shown her. The investigator also recovered several digital cameras from Phillip's bedroom. He then showed Phillip what he was taking, listed the items on a receipt, and gave a copy of the receipt to Phillip.

The investigator handcuffed Phillip and led him out to his unmarked car. Burt and Liz followed the car to the county jail, where Mr. Pierson had agreed to hold Phillip until the next morning. They didn't want him to warn Radovich.

On the way, Liz called Steve to tell him the results of the evening, and that Burt had kept her safe.

Phillip called his attorney, and the attorney told him not

to answer questions, and that he'd see him first thing the next morning. Thank goodness he had a lazy attorney.

On the way to the D.A.'s office, Burt told Liz, "We have more to talk about in the morning. Rudy didn't go to his children's daycare operation today. He drove to an old, run-down motel about thirty miles west of here, just over the Ohio state line. I think that's where he's using the older girls."

"Oh, Burt. I'm so glad we have you working with us. You're amazing! I wondered where those other girls in his files had disappeared to."

Burt called Tom Pierson, and they agreed to meet at the Sheriff's Office the following morning. Liz would still meet Radovich at Majestic Modeling at ten o'clock, and once Radovich left, Burt would pick up Liz to accompany him on the raid of the fake child daycare operation. The search warrants were already issued for both the child daycare raid, and also for the Majestic Modeling studio, once Radovich was in custody.

Tom Pierson told Liz that she would be officially back on his staff as soon as Burt picked her up the next morning.

12

Major Sting

Liz showed up at Majestic before ten that Saturday morning. She was wearing her hidden microphone, and Burt was just around the corner to record everything. Liz walked down the hall to the back room where Radovich was working, "I didn't expect you here so early," he said to Liz, looking up from what he was doing when she walked in. "How did things go with Phillip last night?"

"You sent me over there to have sex with the guy, Rudy, you should have at least told me that!" Liz said, showing as much anger and betrayal as she could muster.

Rudy looked a little taken aback by her outburst. "I thought it was implied."

"No, it wasn't! You said he was going to be taking partially nude shots!"

"Hey!" Radovich shot back. "I know you're not that innocent! Are you saying you've never had sex on a shoot before?"

"That will be right, Rudy! I'm a professional model, not

a prostitute. Jeez, what kind of an operation are you really running here?"

Radovich looked at Liz for a brief minute, and Liz thought she saw a little bit of panic beginning to set in. Had he assumed wrong? He thought she was old enough to read between the lines, but had he been mistaken? Would she run off and tell?

"Hey, listen, I'm sorry I didn't mention it. Some of these customers like to "play around" a bit at the shoots. It adds to the fun. Why do you think they pay so much? I bet you never got paid what I'm paying you at any of your 'professional modeling' shoots. Am I right?"

"I guess you're right about that. I just thought you had some high-level clients who like to look at our bodies, I didn't think it would include going all the way."

"Well, now you know, Liz. You could make a lot of money at these shoots if you open your mind to it," Radovich said, seeming to relax seeing that Liz was now calm and thinking about it. "I told you he was impressed by your photos. So, were you able to make him happy, at least?"

"I think I did, Rudy. I was just taken aback by it all, but I think I did."

Radovich smiled. "I guess you wore him out because I called him this morning, but he didn't answer. He must still be sleeping. Good job, Liz. Here is the $250 I promised, and another $200 for being a good sport and working today."

Liz took the money and tucked it into her jeans pocket. "Thanks, Rudy. I'll see you later?"

"Yes. I'll be late again. Just lock up at three o'clock. And…

thanks, Liz." Rudy gave Liz a knowing smile, but Liz thought, *'Wait until you see me later.'*

Rudy left, and Burt pulled up two minutes later. He had a different car than the one before, the third in three days. "Just how many cars do you own, Burt?" Liz asked Burt when he came into the studio.

"I own seven, but I buy them at the police auctions. When I tail someone, I like to change cars as often as possible."

"That's smart. I can see why Mr. Pierson likes having you on surveillance jobs. But now, let's go and close down a daycare center. And did you get my conversation with Rudy?"

"That was a very short but revealing conversation. Well played, Liz. You sounded genuinely upset about last night."

"That was easy. I hate what he's doing to these girls. There's no doubt what Rudy expected would happen last night."

"I don't know if all the recordings can be used in evidence. That'll be up to the judge. But when we replay those recordings for Rudy, once he's in custody, who knows what he might say?"

Burt drove out east of Erie, near the New York state border. They met the rest of the team at a shopping mall near the highway. The Sheriff's Office and the State Police Emergency Response Team were on hand, as well as an FBI Agent. A female plain-clothes officer had been stationed on a park bench within sight of the house where the children were being housed, and that officer reported that Radovich had just pulled into the driveway.

The entire team headed to the house, and the officer in charge of the operation asked Liz not to enter the house until they called for her. When they pulled up in front, there was a sign on the front lawn which read, '*SAVE THE CHILDREN.*' How ironic!

Liz asked Burt, "Did they put that sign up as a joke?"

Burt said, "I asked around the village, and many people think this place is housing Asian orphans. They think it has some religious affiliation. I guess Radovich thinks that's a good cover for what happens here."

"The more I see of these traffickers, the sicker they make me. The woman I uncovered back in West Virginia a few years ago was drugging girls and selling them to brothels. Her local neighbors thought she was counseling young alcoholics."

The house Burt had traced Radovich to over several days, was a large, three-story, Colonial-style house in disrepair. The steps leading up to the large front porch were rotting, and several of the screens on the windows were torn. Although Burt estimated that there were at least twelve young children, mostly girls, living in the house, they saw no signs of toys or even a swing set outside. In fact, over the several days that Burt had been watching the house, he said he never saw any of the children outdoors, except when they were being led to and from the little bus.

The State Police team surrounded the house while the FBI Agent went to the front door. The bus and Radovich's car were both in the driveway. When the agent knocked on the door, an older Asian lady answered. The agent spoke with her and showed her his badge, but the lady just turned and spoke to someone inside the house. An older Asian man then appeared in the doorway and spoke briefly to the agent before inviting the agent inside. At that point, the agent motioned for the State Police investigators to go inside with him.

Will Lempke was the FBI agent who went inside the house where Radovich was keeping the Asian children that day. The two adults who ran the house seemed friendly. The woman did not speak English, and the man spoke in what came out as broken but good English.

Once inside, Will Lempke and the three investigators who had followed him inside studied their surroundings, looking for any sign of the children. It all seemed so quiet for a house full of children.

"We understand that you have a lot of young children living here. It's awfully quiet for a house full of children, where are they? Where are the children from, and why are they here?"

"Many girls from Asia, two from Moldova. Two Asian boys. Refugees for rehabilitation," the man answered. Will noticed that the man had purposefully left out where the children were, but he kept on with his questions.

"It has been noticed that your bus is dropping the children off at different homes in the area and leaving them there unsupervised. What is the purpose of those visits?" the agent continued.

"Teaching English. Reading and playing games," the man answered.

Just then, a State Trooper came in from the back door, leading Rudy Radovich. "Agent Lempke, this man was leaving out the back door."

"And who are you, sir?" Agent Lempke asked.

"My name is Rudy Radovich. I occasionally volunteer at this charity," Radovich said.

"You must volunteer quite often. We understand you're here almost daily, even driving the bus to deliver the children. What are you doing here all day, and why are you dropping the children off at different places each day?"

"The shelter is short of money, so many residents invite the children to stop by for meals," Radovich responded.

"That's a little different than what this gentleman described," Agent Lempke said. Lempke noticed the cold stare Radovich aimed at the Asian man.

"If you're just a volunteer, then who owns or manages this house? Who is paying the rent and other expenses?" Agent Lempke continued.

"As I said," Radovich continued, "I'm just a volunteer. I have no idea who's in charge."

"Well, if you volunteer, then you must know who agreed for you to be helping here."

"I don't know who's in charge, I told you. Now, I really must leave. I have a business to run back in Erie."

"I understand that, Mr. Radovich. We're very familiar with Majestic Modeling. It appears that you, or possibly your business, are the ones paying for the rent and expenses for this house. You even own that small bus out in the driveway. I think you had better start giving us a little more information here."

"Why do you think that I pay the bills here?" Radovich said, but his wavering voice betrayed his concern.

"We'd also like to know what the contents of the cargo containers were, which you received in Long Beach. The contents were transported to this address, and you paid those invoices as well."

"Just what are you insinuating? I just run a small modeling and photography business."

Then Agent Lempke turned back to the Asian man and asked, "Sir, do you and this lady have any identification papers?"

The man looked pleadingly at Radovich, who seemed to ignore him. He then said, "No, sir. We have no such papers."

"And how long have you been in the United States?"

"Not two years," the man answered.

"Who pays for your services?" Lempke asked.

"I get no pay. I live here and take care of girls and boys."

"Someone must buy the food, clothes for the children, and everything else. Where does the money come from?" Lempke continued.

"I just give bills to Mr. Rudy," the man said.

Agent Lempke had heard enough, so he changed his approach. "We know that these children are being used for illegal sexual activities. We know that Mr. Radovich is running and paying for this operation. We want to help these children. Will you help us?" he asked the Asian man.

"How can you accuse me of such a crime? I won't stand for this," Radovich said, angrily.

Lempke motioned to one of the investigators, signaling that it was time to bring Liz inside.

A few minutes later, Liz walked through the front door,

and Radovich's face went from confusion to terror in a matter of a few seconds.

"Thanks for waiting outside, Miss Thomas," Agent Lempke said to Liz. "Mr. Radovich seems to be denying any involvement here, other than being a volunteer. Can you explain to Mr. Radovich why we think that this is his illegal sex-trafficking operation?"

"I'm sorry, Rudy, but I got a little nosy after the job you sent me to, I guess," Liz started. "I found some pictures in your file cabinets that disturbed me. Some of them probably showing these little girls you have upstairs, unclothed and with adult hands on their bodies."

"You snooping little snake!" Rudy spat his words out at Liz. "You broke into my files?"

"No. I only looked in the drawers you left open. I saw that hard drive, and then I really got nosy. Maybe you can accuse me of snooping on that one. But I was able to open the files in that drive, and I started seeing invoices where you paid for people in containers. I think there may also be invoices for this place you're running here."

"I will certainly be filing charges against you, Liz. I thought I could trust you! Turns out I was wrong. And now, I think I want to speak to my attorney," Radovich stated strongly.

"I'm not sure I would press charges if I were you," Liz said, stepping closer to Radovich. "From what I hear, you're going down. Prostitution is bad enough, Rudy, but child porn...? Now that's just terrible. What you are doing with these little ones upstairs is unforgivable. I'm thinking there is already a warrant out to confiscate everything at Majestic and to search this place, so yes, you need a lawyer. That is if you can find one sleazy enough to even want to touch you."

"You traitor!" Rudy shouted, lunging at Liz, who backed away. One of the officers grabbed Rudy. Rudy violently snatched his arm from the officer's grip. "You'll never work again in this town, Liz! I'll make darn sure of that. I paid you well so you could afford a roof over your head, and this is how you repay me? You're not even that good a model, and you're a lousy employee! You'll pay for this, Liz Thomas!

Agent Lempke stepped in at this point, "Place this man under arrest," he said to one of the troopers who was now standing in the doorway behind Rudy. "And please be sure to read him his rights, with several witnesses. We don't want him getting off on a technicality."

Liz smiled as she watched Radovich being led outside. Then she saw the Asian man looking at her. She expected to see fear or even anger, but instead, she saw what looked to her like relief.

"And what about these two?" one of the troopers asked, looking at the man and woman who ran the house.

Lempke looked at the man and asked, "Are you willing to help us work with these children? We may need your help to talk to some of them."

"Yes," the man quickly said. "I need you to understand our children."

"Okay then. We will have to notify the INS about your status. But we will tell them you are cooperating with us."

"I-N-S?" the man asked.

"Immigration and Naturalization Service. You are not in

the United States legally. So, I have to report it. But if you help us with these children, we will ask the INS Officers to help you," Lempke said.

"Thank you, Mr. Agent. We want to keep our children safe."

Agent Lempke was having a hard time trying to understand this man's concern for the children, knowing that he and Radovich had been delivering them to pedophiles to be abused.

"Take them down to the station for questioning," Agent Lempke said to the trooper.

13

Majestic Modeling

After leaving the raid at the daycare, Burt gave Liz more details about the motel, located in the opposite direction, west of Erie. "I'm glad I decided to tail Radovich one more day. I expected to tail him out here to the daycare, but instead, he headed west. Just over the border into Ohio, there's a very rural area there, with no real cities to speak of. Just lots of vineyards. Several old motels cater to transient workers on construction projects, highway jobs, and so forth. Rudy went to one of those motels and I could tell it isn't being used by those construction guys. Those guys tend to have barbeque grills out front and junk laying around. Instead, I saw frilly girl stuff hanging on a clothesline out back. Radovich went into the office and came out with a young guy, maybe in his early thirties, long ponytail. I parked around the back and saw several young girls, older teens, hanging personal laundry on a clothesline. I didn't want to blow my cover, so I just kept moving. Maybe an hour later, Radovich left, and I followed him back to Majestic. I'd lay odds that those girls are working for Radovich and that the young guy is the 'stable master'."

"I bet you're right, Burt. Did the girls all look to be over eighteen?"

"I guess that the ones out back, hanging laundry, were over eighteen, or close to it. No telling who else might be inside."

"I guess we'll need to get Mr. Pierson working on this one next. It's out of our jurisdiction, but he'll know who to call in Ohio. I wonder how we can bust that place now that Rudy is in custody? It'll need to be quick. We need to raid it before they move those girls to another place."

Liz knew that most of what she had learned during her short employment at Majestic Modeling could not be used as evidence, despite her leave of absence. Radovich's lawyer would call it entrapment, she assumed. However, the District Attorney had a search warrant for Radovich's business and residence, as well as the home where the children were kept. The hard drive was confiscated and the records in those files were very damning. The photos were also damning, but Radovich had been careful not to show faces in most of the nude shots. Luckily, the Federal Statutes on Child Exploitation and Obscenity are very broad, and Liz was sure that Radovich was not getting away with any of this.

As far as Radovich knew, when Liz walked into the daycare where he was housing the young, trafficked kids, she was just a whistle-blower. Liz was going to step away and let the legal system take over.

Because Liz was concerned for the victims, she asked Mr.

Pierson if she could give this news to the family of the young girl who had started this investigation.

"Of course, Liz. That would be wonderful. I was going to call them, but I think hearing the details of Radovich's downfall from you, will be better appreciated by Mrs. Jandra. She really trusted you."

"There may be a few tears shed, but I want them to know that Rudy didn't get away with what happened to their daughter. I just wish we had more details about the guy that raped their daughter. And what do you think we need to do with Tiffany's family, the girl who committed suicide?"

"I've given that a lot of thought, Liz. Her parents are probably not aware of the events that led her to take her own life. Although they are in turmoil right now, I don't think that knowing their daughter's death was probably caused by rape, would ease their pain. We have no evidence to file charges in that case, so I think it will be best for the parents not to know about Majestic. What do you think?"

"With that explanation, Mr. Pierson, I guess I have to agree. Knowing what their daughter went through might just make it worse for them."

"One thing bothers me though. That young boy who was recruiting these girls for Radovich; we need to do something about him. Wasn't it Lenny?"

"I'm so glad you feel that way. As you said before, we may not be able to find him criminally culpable, but somehow, we need to make him understand the consequences of his actions. He wasn't actively pimping those girls, but he was a pimp's agent, for lack of a better term."

"Give that situation some thought, Liz. If you can find a way for us to get through to him, please let me know. We cannot break the law, but somehow, we need to try to straighten that kid out."

"So, I'm officially back on the payroll? If so, can I ask for a couple days off?" Liz said with a chuckle.

"Just so you know, I never actually filed your Leave of Absence request. Seeing we won't need your testimony to get Radovich, I'm throwing out that request. You did more for the D.A.'s office while working at Majestic than if I had kept you in the office. So, if your time off is to get back on the good side of Steve, I'd be happy to grant your request."

"Yes, I need to thank Steve for putting up with my recent antics, and seeing I was still gainfully employed here, as well as taking Radovich's daily pay, I can afford to take Steve out to the Cracker Barrel."

"If you're short on money, I can help you get him a better dinner than at Cracker Barrel."

"I have an ulterior motive calling me over to Cracker Barrel. I'm not sure if I'm ready to share that with you just yet. But how do you hire our legal assistants and paralegals?"

"We've hired a lot of them from local colleges. Why do you ask?"

"Have you ever considered a Work-Study program with Gannon?"

"It's never been asked before, but if the candidate is good, I don't see why we couldn't do that. I'm thinking you may have someone in mind, so have them send me their transcripts and a C-V."

"Thank you. I will."

Tom Pierson had a large smile on his face as Liz left his office. He knew he had one great Assistant D.A. working for him.

"And Mr. Pierson, we need to talk with Burt about another location where he tailed Radovich. I think Burt found the brothel where Rudy was using his older girls. I'm going to see if our 13-year-old can confirm it, now that she'll know that Majestic Modeling is closed down."

"Yes, let's talk after your days off," Pierson said.

Liz called Linda's mom, Valerie, to tell her about the closing of Majestic Modeling. She also told Valerie that she was an Assistant DA. Valerie was thankful that Liz had kept her daughter out of such trouble. She was even more grateful that she had gotten Linda a job interview for the house-cleaning job with Mrs. Behrendt.

"She called me, and I'm meeting her tomorrow with Linda. I'd like to tell Linda how important it was for you to be concerned about her welfare. I did a little research on Google, starting with your guy, Steve. I figured out who you were, but because you kept that secret, I assumed you were doing something undercover, now that this is out in the open, can I tell Linda what a good thing you did for her?" Valerie asked Liz.

"Let's hold off on that for a few more days," Liz said. "I want the Juvenile Offender Officer to question that kid, Lenny. I don't know how culpable he is in this operation, but he was the one who brought many of these girls to Majestic." Liz wanted to say that if Lenny was the one who brought

Tiffany to Radovich, then Lenny was morally responsible, even though he may not be criminally responsible for her death. However, that thought was not something she could share.

"Also, Valerie. My boss, the District Attorney, wants to see your resume and transcript. Our office has openings for paralegals, and Mr. Pierson said he would consider a work-study position for you if you would agree to stay with the D.A.'s office for some time after graduation. Would you be interested?"

"Interested? My God, Liz! I can't believe you did this. How can I ever thank you? You didn't tell me you were working for someone like that when we met, but I had my suspicions, as I told you."

"Mr. Pierson said you might be working for me if this all happens. I can be a tough taskmaster, so just be warned," Liz fibbed.

"I think I can deal well with a tough boss. Remember, I'm working at Wal-Mart and Cracker Barrel."

"Oh yes. That's right! Maybe I'm not that tough after all. Oh, by the way, are you working at Cracker Barrel tonight? I might treat Steve to a trucker's meal."

"Liz, I'm sure you have better places to have dinner. You don't need to go there because of me."

"But that's just the point, Valerie. We like to eat with people we like. So, what time is slow, so we don't get you into trouble if we talk to you?"

"If you come in at seven-thirty, I get off at eight-thirty, and I'll buy you a drink after dinner. How does that sound?"

"Sounds perfect. We'll see you around seven-thirty."

Before Steve and Liz met Valerie, they drove to Liz's rooming house, where Liz introduced Steve to Mrs. Behrendt and paid her for another week of rent. When she told the older woman about Majestic Modeling being closed, Mrs. Behrendt seemed visibly pleased. Liz then went on to tell her that she was moving to a new apartment, closer to her new job, and wouldn't be living in the rooming house anymore. Liz didn't feel it was necessary to give Mrs. Behrendt the details.

Liz also told Mrs. Behrendt that she had spoken to Linda's mother and knew about their meeting for the house cleaning job the next day. Liz asked her to let her know if the cleaning job with Linda worked out well. Mrs. Behrendt assured Liz that she would, and thanked Liz for getting them acquainted.

On their way to Cracker Barrel, Liz told Steve that she had the next two days off, and had some tough assignments to accomplish, which might require some very serious hugging time when he came home.

"So, this one wasn't physically dangerous, but it still damaged you emotionally? What am I going to do with you, miss Trent?"

"Just keep loving me, I guess," Liz answered.

The next day, Liz called Mrs. Jandra, the mother of the thirteen-year-old girl who was raped in one of Radovich's fake photo shoots. She first met Mrs. Jandra when the parents came to the District Attorney's office hoping to file charges against Majestic Modeling. Mrs. Jandra met her husband at the University when she was studying Advertising. Mr. Jandra's family was originally from India, and he was also at

Gannon, getting his master's degree in Bio-Engineering. They had four children, Elisa being the oldest. Elisa was beautiful and photogenic. She had been lured into Rudy Radovich's modeling scheme like all the others, and the parents had been unaware of what was happening to their daughter.

Elisa had originally visited one of Rudy's customers for a photo session one afternoon, which ended up with some nude photos. This had occurred on a boat out in Lake Erie. Although their daughter said she was embarrassed, the man showed her other nude photos he had taken of other girls, so she felt it was just an expected part of the modeling job, and she became comfortable with the man touching her since he said it was necessary to properly position her for the pictures. The second visit to the same customer was much the same. The man began caressing her entire body with oil. She said she was uncomfortable with what was happening, but he also had excited her. On the third visit, Elisa went on the boat and found one of her friends from school was already aboard. They went out on the lake, and this trip ended up with the man removing his clothes to take pictures of himself with the girls. He showed them similar pictures, hoping that they would agree. The man started to have sex with her friend, who started screaming. When Elisa tried to object, the man hit her, and she didn't remember what had happened after that. She woke up in a different place, no longer on the boat, and an older girl was trying to calm her. She was very sore and bleeding from her vagina.

To avoid trouble, the man called Radovich. Radovich came to a remote boat dock to take Elisa. When Elisa did not return home, her parents called her friends and their neighbors. The parents finally reported their daughter as missing. The phone calls resulted in finding that one of the Jandra girl's best friends had also disappeared. The police searched and found no trace of either girl. Elisa's friend was later found dead in the harbor. Three months later, Elisa was found on a road in Ohio one evening and taken to a medical facility. After she went home, she told her parents about the repeated rapes out in the countryside.

The parents told the police and later attempted to press charges against Majestic Modeling. But then they found out that their daughter would have to appear in court against Radovich and his client, and so they decided not to put their daughter through that ordeal and humiliation.

Liz wanted to meet with Mrs. Jandra alone so she could talk more freely. Mrs. Jandra had expressed her trust in Liz's demeanor during their interviews in the D.A.'s office, and Liz wanted the family to know that Radovich was out of business and would probably be in prison for a long time. However, Liz knew that Mrs. Jandra wanted the man who first raped her daughter to pay for what he had done.

Mrs. Jandra greeted Liz at the door and invited her inside her home. After offering Liz a mug of chai tea, she sat down across from Liz. Liz took a sip from the mug and set it down on the coffee table.

"How is your daughter doing?" Liz asked Mrs. Jandra.

"She's doing as well as she can under the circumstances," Mrs. Jandra replied.

Mrs. Jandra went further and thanked Liz for the referral

she gave her daughter to a child counselor. She told Liz that the counseling was helping, but that their daughter was still waking up screaming several times each week. Mrs. Jandra told Liz that her daughter had also suffered from drug withdrawal because her captors were drugging her to keep her compliant. Liz thought, *'The memories will never be entirely gone.'*

"Mrs. Jandra, I thought you should know that we have closed down Majestic Modeling, and Radovich will probably get a long prison sentence. It wasn't for what he did to your daughter, but we also found his involvement in a major, international trafficking operation, and I don't believe he can escape those charges."

"But what about that Hendrickson guy? The man with the boat who destroyed my daughter? Is he also going to prison?" Mrs. Jandra said as tears started to flow.

"He wasn't part of the operation we just busted, but I didn't know his name until you just mentioned it. Tell me what you know about this Hendrickson guy?"

Liz noted everything that Mrs. Jandra told her and then said, "I'll do my best to get this man punished, Mrs. Jandra. I don't know how just yet, but I also don't want him to get away with what he's done."

About a half hour after Liz first arrived at the Jandra residence, Mrs. Jandra was seeing her off. Mrs. Jandra stopped at the door and gave Liz a tight, tearful hug.

"Liz, you were the only bright spot in this terrible situation. I know that the police and District Attorney had to follow their rules, but we so badly wanted revenge against these two men, and we couldn't make it happen, so thank you!"

"I feel your pain, Mrs. Jandra. I wanted that revenge as well. The rule of law is hard to bend. But a few more questions. Do you know how your daughter found Majestic Modeling? Did someone introduce her to Radovich?"

"I don't think she ever mentioned that. I can find out. Is it important?"

"Actually, it is. I think I see a pattern in how the girls got to Majestic, and I want to see if it was the same for your daughter."

"I'll be sure to let you know," Mrs. Jandra said.

"And one more thing. Please ask your daughter if she met any other girls at Majestic and if she knows any of their names. They might have been at that place in the countryside that she mentioned. We may have found where they kept your daughter for those months."

"I'll tell her that this will help you, Liz. She'll want to help you if she can. As time passes, I think she is remembering more details. We think that's what causes her to scream in her sleep."

Liz was driving home when she got a phone call from Burt. She pulled over and parked so she could talk to him. "So, are you reading my mind now, Burt?" Liz teased Burt when she answered the phone. "I was going to call you when I got home."

"I'm just checking up on the star attraction," Burt said, laughing.

"Liz laughed too. "So, what's going on," she asked Burt.

"Well, I just spoke with Tom, and he cannot stop talking about the job you did with Majestic Modeling. But please, don't tell him that I spilled the beans. He doesn't want his Assistant D.A.s to know that he likes them."

"I'll keep it a secret, Burt. But thanks for telling me."

"So, you said that you were going to call me. What's up?"

"It's a bit sensitive. Can I invite you to dinner with Steve and me, so we can discuss it? Pick a night when you aren't tailing somebody."

"I'd never turn down a chance to see you guys again. I'm actually in a dry spell, so, would tonight be okay?"

"Tonight is perfect. Do you like Valerio's? Maybe six-thirty?"

"I'll be there. Looking forward to it. I haven't seen you in almost 24 hours. I'm in withdrawal."

Liz laughed and hung up the phone.

Liz had just pulled into the parking lot of their apartment building when Tom Pierson called her. "The boss is calling me on my day off. Not fair!" Liz said, answering Tom's call.

"I guess I had that coming. Sorry. But I want to run something by you."

"Oh, boy! This sounds serious," Liz said.

"It just might be serious, which is why I wanted to give you time to think about this before you come back. The State Police Crisis Unit is still out at the house with those kids and the two Asian adults. They're having trouble communicating, not just with language, but they cannot figure out the role those two adults played in all this. An investigator with the State was looking through the file when she saw your resume and your experience working with sex traffickers and their victims. She called me to ask if I would let you help her. I told her you had a few days off, and she said she could wait."

"I can go tomorrow, Mr. Pierson."

"No, Liz. I promised you some time off. I told the investigator, and she agreed to wait."

"No. I'm going. I'll take those days off when this is done. We need to get those kids settled as soon as possible. Call her and tell her I'll be there about eight-thirty tomorrow. Is it okay if I stay at a hotel out there until we're done? It'll let me avoid driving each way until we're done. I may need to have Steve stay out there a couple of times too. Is that okay?"

"Of course, expense a hotel. And give my apologies to Steve. And thank you, Liz."

"Not a problem, Mr. Pierson. If those kids need help, I want to be there."

14

Burt - Hendrickson Pay-Back

Liz and Steve walked into their favorite restaurant, which had only been used as a meeting place while Liz was working at Majestic. They told the host they were meeting someone, and he pointed them to a table near the back, "Burt's been here waiting for you. I didn't know that you were friends of Burt's?"

Liz walked up to Burt and gave him a big hug and a kiss on the cheek.

Burt said, "Watch out there, young lady. I don't want this fella here to get the wrong idea."

Steve smiled and grabbed Burt's outstretched hand with his two hands, "Well, thank you, Burt, for keeping this crazy lady safe."

"Crazy? Watch out! I'll make you suffer, buddy," Liz quickly quipped.

"You two have to be the nuttiest couple I've met in a long time. You're both a bit crazy, but I like you guys."

The three sat down for dinner and started to talk. "So, what's the new mission you have me pegged for?" Burt asked.

"Just being upfront, Burt, Tom Pierson is not aware of this conversation. I will be personally paying your fees on this one."

"I'm not sure your money is any good here. Let's hear what you have."

"Well, I *will* pay you. But you remember the young girl that started this whole Majestic investigation? She was brutally raped and then held for three months. I just found out the name of the guy that started it all. His name is Cecil Hendrickson. He calls himself an art dealer, but he seems to like abusing young girls when he can. The girl he raped will not testify against him, so we can't get him on that. But I don't think she was the first or the last. What can I do, Burt? I can't let him get away with it."

"I'm aware of Cecil's reputation. I knew he lured young, 20-something girls to his apartment from the local bars, and in the summer, he took them out on his boat, but I didn't realize he was also preying on these younger girls. How old was she?" Burt asked.

"Thirteen when it happened. He used the same nude modeling ploy. When she objected to his manhandling, he raped her out on his boat. Then Radovich took her away, probably to that motel you found over in Ohio, to keep her mouth shut. And now I suspect that Hendrickson may be responsible for the death of that young girl found out in the harbor this summer."

"I know one of the bars where he hangs out. Nobody likes the guy, and the bartenders are always amazed that the girls will leave with him. Let me see what I can do. Okay?"

"Keep me informed," Liz said.

"Maybe it's better that I don't keep you informed on this one."

"Don't get yourself into trouble, Burt."

"As they say, there are many ways to skin a cat. You should know me well enough by now, that I won't get into trouble. I'll just tell you when it's done. So, now let's change the subject. What's going to happen with that motel operation?"

The mention of a motel operation caught Steve's attention. He looked up from his menu. Flashes of the week when Liz had been kidnapped in a failed bust played through his mind. He recalled it all, the trafficking operation, Liz being transported several states away into a motel being used as a front for a brothel.

"Liz, don't tell me," Steve said. "You don't plan on going into that one?"

"Probably not. But I want to hear what Burt thinks."

"Just so you know, Burt. Liz got drugged, transported across state lines, and ended up in a hotel room with a guy, but was lucky enough to escape."

"I got the customer to take my drugged booze, and it was a motel room," Liz said. "And I escaped."

"Minor details," Steve replied with a scoff. "But she was

tranquilized, and she keeps trying to get herself killed. That's my point."

"Not so loud, Steve," Liz whispered. "The people here already know we're different, but I don't want them to think we're totally nuts."

"I wouldn't suggest that Liz be involved in this. We need a guy to go in as a customer," Burt said.

"I know someone with a lot of that experience," Steve said.

"Wait right there, buddy. You're a civilian," Liz nearly yelled.

"And so are you!" Steve said, matching her tone. "You used me twice before in that role, and you know I wasn't in any danger."

"Tell me more," Burt said. "This is interesting, and it just might work. We need to act fast before that guy over in Ohio finds out that Radovich has been arrested. Tomorrow is a holiday, right? Can we plan something quick?"

They ordered and ate their meals, while Liz glared at Steve. Steve saw the glares and figured this was payback for her, always keeping him worried. Liz had her Chinese kids on her mind, and now Steve was trying to play detective without her.

The next morning, Burt was talking to a friend of his who was with the Ohio State Police. He told them about the Majestic Modeling operation and that there was suspicion of some underage girls from that Erie-based trafficker being used in a motel brothel in Ohio. He further explained that they needed to act quickly before word reached the motel manager about Radovich's arrest. If Burt could get a fake customer to get into the stable and pay for an underage girl, would Ohio Police cooperate to make arrests?

It turned out that Ohio investigators had been watching that operation but had no evidence other than one-on-one prostitution, which was difficult to prosecute, so they told Burt they would certainly cooperate to close down the operation if they could prove that underage girls were being used there.

Then Liz got a call from Mrs. Jandra telling her that she had spoken with her daughter. Her daughter had gone to Majestic Modeling with a boy named Lenny. Elisa also remembered two girls from her high school who had run away from home, and they had cared for her at that place when she was hurt. Both girls were sixteen, and she thought their names were Alexia, known as Lexy, and the other was Beth. They were pretty wild. Her daughter said she saw them at Majestic talking with Radovich and a younger man. They both got into a car with the young man. The next time Elisa saw them was at a place in the country. They were kind to her when the men hurt her.

Liz passed this information on to Burt, and Burt told Steve to listen for those names when he went to the motel. Because Steve was afraid that Liz would want to be involved in this operation, he reminded her that she was an Assistant D.A. in Pennsylvania and getting involved in an Ohio sting was a conflict that could get both her and Tom Pierson in trouble.

Liz told Steve, "So, you're starting to use the law against me now? I've taught you too well. Wait until I get you home."

Steve said, "Promise?"

Burt met Steve at a service station about a mile from the motel in Ohio. Burt rigged Steve up with his mini-microphone and then discussed how Steve was going to get inside and talk with the girls. When the Ohio state police arrived, Burt and Steve explained the situation to the officers. Burt showed them the recording equipment, and they agreed that Steve would tell them when to come unless they could hear that Steve was in trouble.

Burt stayed in the back seat of the unmarked patrol car, and Steve drove to the motel. Steve went into the office and rang the bell using the small 'Ring for Service' cowbell on the desk. A young man, late-twenties, or early thirties, looking quite bedraggled, came in from the back room. "Well, hello," the young man said, greeting Steve. "What can I do for you on this fine day? Driving through for the holiday?"

"Actually, I'm working at the shipyard in Erie for a couple of weeks, but they aren't working this weekend because of the holiday. I was hoping to find a nice girl to spend the afternoon with."

"Not sure why you stopped here. You can find all the girls you want on the beach on a day like this."

"The guys in the yard said Rudy always sent them out here. Maybe I have the wrong place. Sorry."

"They told you about Rudy? What was his last name? Do you remember?"

"Some foreign name. Something like 'vich' on the end?"

"Okay, sure. Rudy Radovich. As long as friends of Rudy sent you, we can take care of you. Are you looking for a few hours or all night?"

"A few hours is fine. But the guys said you specialize in young girls. Is that right? I don't want some old, experienced one. I like young girls. The younger, the better."

"Yep. That's Rudy's specialty. We've got a couple of sixteen-year-olds available. Almost had one fourteen coming, but she got cold feet, Rudy told me."

"Okay. Sixteen will have to do. That fourteen would have been special. How much for the afternoon?"

"Three and a half for the young ones. No rough stuff, you hear. Rudy doesn't allow rough stuff with these young ones. To each his own, I guess. I prefer the twenty-year-old we have. She's been around here since she ran away from home. Been here five years. She can teach you things. She was just giving me some lessons in the back room."

How very unprofessional, Steve thought, looking at the man in disgust. *I bet Rudy wouldn't be too happy to find out he's letting the girls give him lessons.*

"Alright. Here's the three-fifty. Where do I find her?" Steve said, handing the man the money.

"Here's the key to Room #8. I'll send Lexy down in a minute. Go get comfortable."

Steve took the key and walked around the corner from the front desk and through the long hall to Room #8. He was surprised that his and Burt's plan to use Rudy's name had worked so easily.

Steve had to wait less than five minutes before there was a knock on the door. Steve opened it and was surprised to see a girl with a sneer on her face. She did look young, but certainly not innocent. And fearless.

"So, you're Lexy? I'm Steve."

"Hi. What are you looking for today? Most want to start with oral. Is that what you want?"

"I was hoping just to talk for a while. Is that okay?" Steve asked.

"If that's how you want to spend your money, that's fine with me, "Lexy responded.

"The man said you were sixteen. Just curious, but why'd you choose this line of work?"

"Hated school. My parents didn't care what I did, and all the boys at school wanted to do was screw around for free. I figured I should get paid for it, right?"

"What about falling in love with a nice guy someday?"

"Don't get all mushy on me. I've never seen anyone say they loved somebody and mean it. They just cheat on one another and fight."

"I guess that you're talking about your parents?"

"Yeah. And for my friend, Beth, it was even worse. Her ol' man's a lush, and he beat up her and her mom all the time. Her mom told Beth to leave home because the guy might kill her someday. We're happy here. Food's good and money in our pocket."

"You didn't look very happy when you walked in."

"Lot of the customers get kinky ideas. I don't like that. Rudy promised the guys would always be gentle with us, but they're not. So, I get a little worried, is all."

"Wouldn't it be nice to find a guy who respected you and always treated you kind and gentle?"

"You ain't offering, are you? You're talking really weird. Maybe we need to get down to business, so you quit talking."

"Well, Lexy. It's Alexia, isn't it? I'm not here for that. If I told you that I'd help to find you a better home, and someone to help you, will you take me up on the offer? I'm not talking about making you go home, but maybe find you a good group home, with other girls for support. Maybe you and Beth could stay together? A life like the one you have here will not be healthy for you, both physically and emotionally. Someday, one of these guys who's too rough might just kill you. I don't want that to happen to you. Understand?"

"But I'm afraid of Mr. Rudy. He won't let me leave. He'd find me."

"Rudy Radovich has been arrested. He'll be in prison for a long time. You'll not have to worry about him anymore. What about this guy running the motel? Are you afraid of him?"

"Eddie's just a mouse. He's okay. He's more afraid of Rudy than we are. He's never hurt us. He's got the hots for that Brenda, and she tells him when to jump and how high."

"So, if Rudy is out of the picture and this motel is being closed down, will you come back to Erie and meet my girlfriend? She's the one who took down Rudy. She'll find a way for you and Beth to feel safe and get some support."

"If this place is closing, then maybe I'd like to meet your girlfriend. Is she as screwy as you?"

Steve simply smiled.

"If this group stuff gets too weird, I'll just run away again," Lexy said.

"I guess that's fair. But I hope you'll give it an honest

effort. Nothing is perfect or easy, so it's also up to you to help the others in a group."

"I'll try, I guess. Nowhere to go if this place is history."

"Don't get scared when I say this, Lexy. Burt, I think Lexy is ready to leave. You can head on over."

"Who's Burt?" Lexy asked.

15

The China Story

Liz was at the house near the Pennsylvania-New York border before eight o'clock the next morning. As was normal, Liz could not sleep when she had victims on her mind. Poor Steve was beside himself with worry about Liz. He told her, "I don't know what I hate worse about your work. The possibility of physical harm is bad enough, but this mental anguish you put yourself through may be just as dangerous." On nights like the last one, Liz had to agree with him.

Liz went into the house and asked the State Trooper, who was drinking coffee in the kitchen, if Laura Griffin, the State's Crisis Team's investigator was there yet. The trooper recognized Liz from the day they closed the house, and he said that Laura had a family issue to deal with and had called to say she'd be there before noon, at the latest.

Liz poured herself a cup of coffee while she waited. She was about to sit down when the Asian man entered the kitchen carrying a tray with dirty bowls, chopsticks, and a few spoons.

The man set the tray down, bowed deeply toward Liz, and said, "Welcome, Miss Liz. Very happy to see you. I understand you want to help my children."

Liz was surprised by the man's remark. She could see that this man cared for these children, but he must have known what they were being used for. How did he justify their abuse in his mind?

Liz responded, "Thank you. Can I ask you your name, please? Maybe we could talk together. Would you like to have some coffee?"

"My name Hu. Hu Yang. I make tea. Yes, then we please talk," he said.

Liz went into the large sitting room, looking out over the front porch. Although the house was sparsely furnished, she could see that everything was neat and extremely clean. She had still not seen or heard the children, but Mr. Pierson had told her there were twelve children in the house, ten girls and two boys. One boy and one girl were from Moldova, and the others were all from China. Although the records showed that two boys arrived from China, only one was found. With all of these people in the house, Liz was amazed that there was no clutter, no dirt, and particularly no noise coming from upstairs.

Hu came into the sitting room with his tea and a plate of small cookies, which he offered to Liz. Liz had not eaten breakfast, so she gladly took a few cookies. Hu remained standing silently. Liz motioned to the chair across from her and said, "Please sit down. Tell me about yourself. Where are you from?"

"Hu Yang from small village near port of Shenzhen in China. I am fifty-eight years and born to farmer family of nine children."

"I thought the Chinese government was restricting the number of children. That is a very large family," Liz said, showing some surprise.

"Yes, those rules are now enforced," Hu said. "I was second youngest of my family's children, and when last child was born, the government said no more to my father. Farmer needed many children for farm."

"And who is the woman I saw with you when I was here? Is she your wife?" Liz asked.

"She is Chu Hua Zhao. We are not man and wife. Chu Hua ran orphanage near my village. She is friend and I helped her there."

"Were these children from that orphanage? I want to understand why they came here, and how they came," Liz continued.

"Yes. Most are from Chu Hua's orphanage. Chinese government did not help to buy food for children. They said we should send them to work or find American families to adopt. We had two small, weak children die. Men came to take children for work, but we saw they were using children's bodies for pleasure."

"I understand," Liz said. "So, you wanted to escape, and try to save them."

"Yes. Find a man working at container port. He say would help. Gather much food as can find and more supplies. Man help us hide these things in a big, metal box. At night, Chu

Hua and I took children, fifteen children, to container port and he lock us inside with our food. In morning, we feel container moving. We are in dark. Only small holes for air or light. We put onto ship."

"Oh my," said Liz. "It must have been so hot in that container. You were lucky to survive."

"Very hot. Hard to breathe. One day loading ship, we think twelve days at sea, but not sure," Hu continued.

"Did you have enough food?" Liz asked. "That's a very long time in that steel box."

"We used all the food with two more days still on ship. Four children die. Chu Hua and me, we stop eating before that. Some children sick because of ocean storm, and they stop eating."

"That must have been just terrible," Liz said, with tears welling up. "What happened after you arrived?"

"We could hear that container was put on truck. The truck took us to country place, like farm. A man opened door, gave us food and water, but we all became sick. He helped us bury dead children. We stay there two days, then he put us in back of truck with food and water. We drive almost three days, then come to this place."

"That's a terrible story, Hu. I know that you wanted to help these children. I know you had no idea how long and terrible that trip would be on the ship. Did you expect that the children would be adopted here? Is that why you came?" Liz asked.

"We hope. Yes. But children were starving in China. We

must try. At least these ten are still alive, have clothes, and enough food," Hu replied.

"Did you know that Mr. Radovich was going to be using the children for their bodies? That is why he is going to prison. That is illegal in the United States," Liz said.

"We did not know. Man in Shenzhen tell us he would get us to United States. No other promise. I only meet Mr. Rudy when truck arrive. I ask him if children be adopted. He tell me it takes time, but children need to earn money. Only difference of life in orphanage and this house is children is not hungry and have clean clothes. But in China, maybe all be dead now, because no food."

At this point, Liz had reached her full crying mode. She couldn't believe that people in this world could abuse young children like these, and she wasn't blaming Chu Hua or Hu, who meant well. How could these children ever recover to lead a normal life?

Hu looked over at Liz with concern. "So sorry, Miss Liz. I did not want you to be so sad."

"That's okay, Hu. I need to understand, so I can try to help. Can you tell me about the children? How old are they? Also, tell me a little about those who died on the ship."

Hu began, "Three children died were youngest. Two girls, three years, one boy four years. Other who die was oldest. He was twelve. Always sick at orphanage. Others are Chinese, nine girls and one boy now healthy, oldest twelve, youngest is six years. Ivan told us one Chinese boy here before, but he gone. Not know where. When arrive, two more children already here. Boy twelve and girl maybe ten years. We not know them much. Girl not talk English. Boy very quiet."

"Why did you help Mr. Radovich? I don't understand," Liz asked.

"Afraid. Safety for children. Sorry, but once try to stop him sending girl out for a man. I know he touches girls. Mr. Rudy tell me if the girl not learn, he send her back to China."

"Hu, please know that these children will not be sent back to China. Miss Griffin and I will find Chinese-speaking people to help them. I also hope we can somehow find families to adopt them."

"Thank you, Miss Liz. I do not think Miss Griffin like my children. She not look at me with eyes like you. I think she believe I bad man, like Mr. Rudy."

"I'm so sorry, Hu. Did you tell her the same story, like you just told me?"

"I try, but she no wants to hear."

"Well, I listened, Hu. And I will do everything I can to keep these children safe. And nobody will use their bodies like that ever again."

"Thank you, Miss Liz. Will Chu Hua and me be sent back to China?"

"Is that what you want, Hu?"

"No. I understand we not wanted here. We will do what told."

"Well, I want you to stay. I will talk to the Immigration man when he comes."

16

Burt - Devious Plan

Lucy was a beautiful Hispanic girl who Burt guessed to be around 23 or 24. She was well-dressed and very classy. Lucy introduced Natalie, a strikingly beautiful black girl, who said she was 27, and then Maggie, a red-headed Irish girl with fire in her eyes. Maggie introduced herself by saying she had heard that this gathering was because "we all want to burn this guy at the stake." Maggie did not disclose her age, and Burt figured he didn't dare ask her.

Burt had arranged the meeting with the ladies after speaking to a bartender at one of the bars frequented by Cecil Hendrickson. This Cecil Hendrickson character, a kid who had inherited his parent's estate at age twenty when they were killed in an Alaskan airplane crash, was responsible for the rape of Mrs. Jandra's thirteen-year-old daughter. Hendrickson, now 32 years old, had never worked a day in his life, from what Burt had dug up about the guy. Yet, he drove a flashy sports car and owned an even flashier yacht. It was bad enough that he attracted the 20-somethings that hung around the hotel bars around the harbor, but now his attentions seemed to have turned toward the early teen girls. Brutalizing a 13-year-old was horrendous in Burt's way of thinking, and Cecil needed to pay for doing it! And now, Liz thought Hendrickson may have killed another young girl.

Burt didn't spend much time in those bars, but he knew the bartenders well because he used their information services in his line of work. Bartenders probably heard more sins than a priest in a confessional, and they had to remain friendly, even with the people they didn't like. So, Burt made the rounds of the Erie hotels, being sure to avoid contact with Cecil. He found out that there were a growing number of disgruntled, 20-something, pretty girls, who had been wined, dined, and sweet-talked into a few nights of sex, then quickly dropped for the next pretty face who Cecil noticed. Several bartenders mentioned that they had overheard a group of those women, saying that they would love to get even. A group of disgruntled women working together was worth meeting, Burt thought.

A few nights before the meeting with the three ladies, Burt had asked one of the bartenders, whom he had tipped well for information in the past, to drop his business card to a couple of the ladies who had mentioned wanting revenge. Two days later, he received a call from Lucinda (Lucy) Chavez, asking if he was the guy wanting to know about Cecil Hendrickson. Burt set up a meeting with Lucy and she asked if she could invite two other friends along. Burt said, "yes." He invited them to Valerio's, where he knew Cecil would never be seen. Burt even dressed up for the occasion.

Now, sitting across from Lucy, Natalie and Maggie, Burt introduced himself.

"My name is Burt Snyder, and I'm a private investigator. I've been working on a pedophile, sex trafficking case here in the Erie area."

"Hey, we're all over twenty-one, Burt. We may have made some bad decisions, but we were old enough to figure we had picked the wrong guy," Lucy said.

"No, I understand," said Burt. "But what would you think if some guy you know had lured at least one, if not more, 13-year-old girls out on that boat of his, and then brutally raped them?"

"He did that?" Natalie asked. "For real? He needs to be castrated."

"I had a bad feeling about him," Maggie said. "I regretted going on that weekend with him, within hours after leaving. His sweet talk in the bar reeled me in, but once we were alone, the only thing on his mind was sex, and he liked it rough, which I hate."

The girls all agreed that was Cecil's style. Then Lucy asked, "So, how do we get him for raping that poor little girl? Shouldn't he be in jail?"

"The only way to do that is to put that girl on the witness stand. After he raped her, she spent almost three months in an Ohio brothel, drugged up, before she got away. We don't want her to be cross-examined by his lawyers. She already has screaming nightmares trying to get over what happened."

"Then why are we here?" Natalie asked. "What can we do?"

"We set him up," Burt said. "Would any of you feel guilty if he went to prison for something he didn't do?"

The three women looked at each other and smiled.

"Hell no!" Lucy replied. "What do you want us to do? If we can get some justice for that little girl, then let's go for it."

"I'm glad to hear that. I'll give you my plan, but don't start working on it until I give you the go-ahead."

Burt looked at the three ladies sitting across the table from him. Their eyebrows were raised in anticipation of what Burt was about to say next. Burt continued, "If the three of you approached Cecil, and offered to give him a three-girl weekend, do you think he'd accept the proposal knowing that he'd dropped each one of you?"

Natalie was the first to speak. "I think Cecil likes kinky, he'd love the idea of getting together with three beautiful girls on his boat for an entire weekend. The thing is this, I don't want any part of him again."

"I understand," Burt said. "All you three will have to do is get aboard his boat. I assume you'd each take a small duffel bag with clothes and toiletries, right?"

The three of them nodded.

"And if I gave you some contraband to hide onboard, could you do that?"

"That'd be easy," said Maggie. "There are lots of small storage spaces onboard."

"Then would one of you be a good actress, feign an accident, requiring a 9-1-1 call?"

Lucy smiled and said, "So, I assume we are planting some

drugs or other incriminating items, then getting off when the ambulance arrives?"

"I didn't mention drugs, but now that you understand, are any of you against the idea?" Burt asked.

"I know that none of us three are users, but I think Cecil has small amounts aboard for those who want it," Maggie said. "If this can get him arrested, I'm for it. But sentences for drug possession are not very long."

"I'm not talking possession. I'm looking for dealing 10-kilos of cocaine, maybe more. Can each of you carry about 12-15 pounds, if I can get that much?"

"My god! How are you going to get that much cocaine?" Natalie asked.

"That's why I need you to wait for me to say I'm ready. I have friends in the right places in the DEA. They know when a shipment is heading in and then they make a bust. They like to find out where the drugs are being delivered, but they seldom find that out. If that delivery ends up on Cecil's boat, and they understand why I'm setting him up, they've still made their drug bust, and we get a pedophile off the street to boot. Nobody likes pedophiles, even other crooks. I can assure you that Cecil will not enjoy his time in prison once the other inmates find out."

"Will that really work, Burt?" Lucy asked. "It seems a little over-the-top."

"I'll talk to my buddy in the DEA. He trusts me. I'm hoping he'll let me explain my idea to his team and tell them why Cecil needs to be taken down. That's the tough part. They haven't seen what this guy has done. If I convince them that he needs to be put away, they will personally hand you the cocaine and watch you take it aboard Cecil's boat. They may even search you when you leave, to be sure the cocaine is never out of their control. Then they will stage the raid on Cecil's boat and find the drugs."

"Won't a good lawyer be able to him off?" Maggie asked. "Then we would've gone through all of this for nothing."

Burt understood their concern and continued to try and assure them that there was no way Cecil would be getting away with any of this.

"What if we find some dealers who tell the DEA that Cecil is their supplier?" Natalie asked. "That might tighten the noose a bit tighter. Do we know any drug dealers that we can trust?"

Everyone laughed, but the ladies all started thinking.

"What devious thinking, ladies," Burt replied. "I hope I haven't corrupted you. But now that we've talked about it, let's all think about it and get back together again. This doesn't need to happen right away. In the meantime, if you see any other possibilities, give me a call. We just need to get Cecil into prison before he ruins the lives of any more girls."

"On that, I think we all agree," said Lucy.

Later, during the same day, Burt went to see Fred, the bartender who had helped him find Lucy. He wanted to thank Fred for getting the ladies to meet with him. Burt had known Fred for several years and had used him as a source of information for several of his divorce cases. He took on such cases when he hit a dry spell and became hungry. Damn, he hated divorce cases, but sometimes he just needed the income.

Fred was one of the older, very professional bartenders in Erie. He had worked in the old, classic Erie hotels, but now, the action was along the waterfront. Fred knew all of the regulars, both men and women, who used the bar to meet people. Some just wanted conversation, but others were looking for a relationship. Most of those relationships lasted one night, but a few ended with a wedding. Because Fred was gray-haired and well-spoken, people trusted him. He knew when to talk, but also knew when to shut up and just listen.

"Hey, Fred. Slow day in here. I'll have one of those draft Porters if you still have it on tap," Burt said as he jumped up onto one of the stools at the bar.

"Yes, very slow for a Thursday. It'll get busier in an hour or so. You're not a regular here, Burt, so what's going on?" Fred responded as he placed Burt's glass of Porter on the bar.

"I just wanted to thank you for putting me in touch with Lucy. She has been very helpful in my investigation."

"I'd forgotten about that," Fred said. "It was about Cecil Hendrickson, right? He has bedded down nearly every young, willing girl in Erie, I think. The word has gotten around though, and the nice women now avoid him like the plague."

"That's what I heard from Lucy and some of her friends. After meeting them, I'm surprised that Cecil was able to seduce them. They were all nice women, not bar flies. I didn't picture any of them just jumping into the sack with anyone who comes along."

"Burt, I've heard Cecil's line more than once. Everyone knows he's got money, and he talks to every one of his conquests like he wants a beautiful wife on his arm. They will be that wonderful Mrs. Hendrickson he's been searching for. After you hear that ploy being used about ten times a month, I roll my eyes. The spiel never changes. I've been tempted to warn some of those nice women when I see them falling for it, but I realize that Cecil could get me fired. Management likes him, of course. He spends a ton of money at the hotel and bar."

"Again, that's sorta' what Lucy and her friends described. But after one weekend with him, they all saw through the BS. Then he just moved on to the next one."

"At one time, I thought there was no end to the line-up of women waiting for Cecil to woo them. But finally, the word has gotten around, and he can't get a nice lady to talk to him as easily as he could before. The other night, Cecil was sitting at the bar crying the blues to some guy I'd never seen before. He mentioned that he couldn't even get a girl from Majestic anymore. He said that Rudy's not answering his phone calls."

"Cecil mentioned Majestic? Did he say anymore?" Burt asked. He had one more piece of the puzzle now, and he was greatly interested to hear more.

"Not Cecil, the other guy said that Majestic had shut down, but he could help Cecil out. He asked Cecil what he was looking for."

"The stranger knew about Majestic. Wow! What did he offer to do?" Burt asked.

"I didn't catch it all, and the guy didn't seem to want me hearing everything, but he asked Cecil a very weird question. If I quite remember, this is what he said verbatim: 'How young are you looking for?'"

Burt winced.

"Yeah. Then I heard Cecil say, 'Rudy sent me a couple virgins. That's what I like.'"

"What did you think he meant by that?" Burt asked.

"Well, that description doesn't apply to the girls I've seen Cecil seducing in here. I guess he was referring to some of the college girls, but these days, even that's a stretch. I'm a little too old to be aware of these things, I suppose, but I didn't like how that conversation was going. I hear some creepy things tending bar, but that conversation sounded bad. When the guy saw me looking, he led Cecil over by the window, so I couldn't hear anymore."

"Would you recognize that stranger enough to describe him, Fred?"

"I can probably do better than that, Burt. That happened last week, but the guy has been in here several times since then. He comes in around seven, talks to all the guys who are in here alone, hands them a business card, and he leaves around nine. He wasn't in here last night, so he might show up tonight. Maybe he's hitting all the bars along the waterfront hotels down here."

"Seven o'clock, you say? Well, it's five-thirty and I could use an early dinner. If I take that booth over there, could you send a waitress over with a menu? If you see that guy walk in, can you give me a wave?"

"I sure will, Burt. I know you're onto something, so, I won't ask. But eventually, I'd love to know what this is all about," Fred said, with a quizzical look on his face.

"You got it. Thanks, Fred. Send the waitress over with

another Porter when she comes. Have her put the two beers on my dinner tab." Then Burt dropped a twenty on the bar and took his half-empty beer over to the booth.

As Fred had suggested, the bar started to fill up around six-thirty when Burt was just finishing his whitefish dinner. He had eaten the Lake Superior whitefish here before, and it was one of his favorites. Burt ordered a Brandy-Manhattan after dinner and was nursing it. He looked over toward the bar, giving Fred an appreciative nod toward his Manhattan, and then saw Fred point toward the door, as a man walked in.

The guy was in his late thirties, Burt estimated. He was clean-cut, well groomed, but dressed casually. He appeared to have decided on a look that would not turn off the rich or the poor; not too flashy but just enough to look like he belonged on one of the local yachts. He immediately went to the bar, ordered what appeared to be a Vodka-tonic, and then started drifting around the bar. He saw two men talking and one of them gave the guy a quick smile and a thumbs up, which the man responded to by raising his glass and nodding.

The guy then started talking to the loners. Some conversations lasted a bit longer than others and ended when the guy handed them a business card. The man was about to leave when he spotted Burt sitting alone in his booth with dirty plates just being taken away. He walked up to Burt, looked him over, and asked him if he was new in town.

"No, I've lived here a few years," Burt responded. "Just don't hang out in the bars much. I was just in the mood for a nice dinner. Sick of my own cooking, I guess."

"What brought you to Erie, may I ask?" the guy asked Burt.

"I was a Marine Sergeant, wounded in Desert Storm, just living off my pension. Too old to start a new career and too young to give up, I guess."

Mind if I sit with you? The man asked Burt. Burt motioned for the man to have a seat and he slid into the seat across from where Burt was sitting. Burt took another sip of his Manhattan and the man continued with his assessment of Burt.

"Not married? It looks like you would have some nice ladies wanting to take care of you," the guy continued. "Just stress the wounded veteran part."

"Not sure how to find women these days. I've been away from that scene too long," Burt responded.

"What are you looking for? Trying to find a wife?" the guy asked.

"Been there, done that. Divorced and want to stay that way," Burt told him.

"You haven't given up yet on companionship, have you?"

Burt was starting to see how smoothly this guy got around to what he wanted. Burt said, "As I told you, I don't know how to approach women anymore."

"I know some nice girls. Maybe I could help you out. Are you looking for an experienced woman or something younger?" the guy asked.

"I'm not looking for some streetwalker if that's what you mean. If I met a nice, clean, younger girl, maybe I'd be interested," Burt said.

"How young do you want? I know somebody with a house full of girls, twelve to thirty. Any of that interesting to you?"

"Twelve? Really? I can't imagine," Burt said.

"Oh, sure. And they're willing to please. These girls are from Russia. They had no food back home and not even a warm place to sleep. They're world-wise and know how to please a man. No strings attached if you understand."

"How do I go about this? This isn't something I've ever done before," Burt said.

"Here's my card. We can talk price, but figure $100 an hour. If you want a longer session, the price per hour is less. I think you'd enjoy the young girls. Call me when you decide, and we can arrange a place for you to meet them."

Burt took the card and tucked it into his shirt pocket. Then he shook hands with the man and watched him get up and walk away. Probably heading to the next bar. After the man left, Burt found himself glued to his seat in shock. You would think the guy was selling paint and not actual humans... young humans to be exact. Cheaper if you bought five gallons instead of just one. Twelve-year-old girls know how to please. Burt thought he was an experienced adult, but what he'd learned in the last few weeks was making him sick.

He finished his drink, waved to Fred, and left the bar. He was going to call Tom Pierson tomorrow and ask what he should do with this newfound information. He didn't sleep well that night, and he started to see why Liz Trent's guy, Steve, was so worried about her. These trafficking situations really messed up one's emotional well-being.

17

Liz and Lenny

Liz knew that she needed to put a stop to Lenny. She wasn't sure how much the young boy knew about what happened to these girls after he delivered them to Radovich. As much as she doubted that he was completely aware of the consequences of his actions, a part of her knew that deep inside, he knew that what he was doing was wrong. How could he bring his classmates, some of whom had crushes on him, to a man who was going to destroy their lives? Liz wanted to get inside Lenny's head.

She had a meeting planned with Tom Pierson to discuss Lenny, and how they should proceed. That morning, when she and Tom met, Tom said he had contacted the Juvenile Correctional Officer and arranged a meeting. He told Liz that the Juvenile Correctional Officer, Laurie Willis, was going to stop by the DA's office around 2 o'clock later that day to discuss Lenny.

Liz returned from lunch, later that afternoon, and started

organizing her thoughts about how to explain the situation to the Correctional Officer. Just before 2 o'clock, she heard a female voice at the reception desk, asking to see Mr. Pierson. Liz grabbed her notes and started towards Pierson's office where a woman in a wheelchair was already wheeling through his office door. Liz stood outside Tom's office and when he noticed her, he motioned for Liz to enter.

"Miss Willis, I'd like you to meet my Assistant District Attorney, Elizabeth Trent. Liz, this is Laurie Willis, the Juvenile Correctional Officer I told you about."

Liz extended her hand and shook Laurie Willis' hand. The woman had a warm and captivating smile and a radiant disposition that made her eyes twinkle. Laurie was a very distinguished-looking black woman, and Liz estimated her to be about 40 years of age. Liz could tell that she had been in a wheelchair for a long time because her legs appeared to have lost muscle definition, and her legs seemed immobile.

"Mr. Pierson spoke highly of you when we spoke this morning, Liz. You recently helped to break up a sex trafficking ring."

Tom Pierson quickly broke in, "Liz didn't just help in this sting, Laurie, she worked undercover, gathered crucial evidence, and even went to a client's home to set up the first arrest. That led to finding a house full of young Asian kids and then to an Ohio motel being used as a brothel. None of this would have occurred if Liz hadn't been on the case."

"Oh, my! You're my kind of hero," Laurie said. "I loved to be involved in surveillance and drug raids until I took a bullet that put me in this contraption. But I still love police work, and this Juvenile job is rewarding if we can turn some of them around."

"I'm so glad to see you think that way, Miss Willis. I see some kids in this case that could use an experienced person to change their life's direction."

"Well, first, call me Laurie. And may I call you Liz? What juvenile issues have you run into? I'm here to help in any way I can."

"First of all, we have a young man named Lenny. I'm not sure that I can say he was criminally involved in this case, but he certainly is morally culpable. He was taking young girls to this modeling agency, for which he was being paid a finder's fee. The man at the modeling agency was telling him what types of girls' bodies he was looking for, and several of the girls have told their parents that Lenny just told them it was modeling for photographs. The photo sessions began innocently but used very revealing costumes. That led to topless, then naked photos. Eventually, the clients fondled the girls, and most were raped. Those that objected were abducted and kept in a motel in Ohio, sold to guys looking for young virgin girls. You may have heard about the recent suicide of the local high school girl, and we believe she was one of the girls that Lenny brought to the modeling agency."

"Oh, my, what a story. I can see why you think there is nothing to arrest this boy for. How old is he, might I ask?"

"Lenny just turned sixteen. He just finished ninth grade."

"And you have statements from some of the girls, or their parents, that Lenny was the one to bring the girls to the modeling agency?"

"Yes, two parents have told me that their daughters said it was Lenny. I didn't want to call the parents of the girl who committed suicide, but I'm quite sure that Lenny was involved there. And by the way, I was working undercover at the modeling agency, so I've seen Lenny at the agency. He once brought a girl while I was there."

"And what happened with that girl?" Laurie asked.

"I told the owner of the agency, who has since been arrested, that the girl was too skinny to be a model. Truth is, she met his criteria perfectly. Then I went behind his back and met with the girl's mother, and we were able to find a different job for her."

"I'm loving how you take charge of situations, Liz. You really go above and beyond," Laurie added.

"Tom Pierson said, "And to be sure she didn't interfere with our case, Liz submitted a leave of absence request before going undercover. She thinks of all the important details."

"Impressive," Laurie said. "But you met this Lenny while you were undercover? Is that right?"

"Yes, just those two times I described."

"Is Lenny aware that you were working undercover, Liz?"

"No. I asked the parents not to mention me to their daughters," Liz answered.

"Here's what I'm thinking, Mr. Pierson. If Liz agrees, I'd like her to approach Lenny, using her previous meetings with him as an excuse to talk with him. Liz and I can work out a potential dialogue, to see how much Lenny knew about the modeling agency, and if he knew about the sexual side of the business. I could then issue a Juvenile warrant for him to be questioned about the criminal activity of people he associated with, such as the owner of the modeling agency."

"Liz, what do you say?" Tom asked her.

"Of course, I'm saying yes. Do I need to take another leave of absence?"

"I think it's too late for that, Liz. We planned this one right here in my office," Pierson said.

"And I see no need to worry about that," Laurie said. "Once Liz finds out how much Lenny knew, she will end up telling him that she met him while working undercover during the sting. Then Liz and I will question Lenny in my office. But Liz, how does a lawyer learn to do everything that you've just described to me?"

"Oh, I was a cop in my previous life. Everything I did back then was undercover. I look younger than my real age, so I was always used as the prey in sting operations. I was getting burned out by seeing all the young people destroyed by these perps, so decided I could lead a much more normal life by prosecuting them."

"And don't forget that young guy who worries about you, and now you've threatened that trust he had in you," Pierson interjected.

"Yes, I have sorta reneged on that promise, haven't I," Liz responded.

"I've got one of those situations as well, so I understand," Laurie said.

"Sounds like a subject for '*girl talk*', now that we'll be working together," Liz said.

"Yes, I think I'll stay out of that one," Tom Pierson said.

"But Liz, you have my permission to work with Miss Willis on the Lenny situation. Just keep me informed. I'll keep your name out of the news until you tell me you have tied up this loose end."

"Thank you, Mr. Pierson. I know I have other responsibilities in the office, and I'll keep on top of those as well."

"Thank you both for taking this on. If we can divert Lenny away from future criminal activity, this is worth the extra time and effort."

Laurie set up an appointment for the next morning to develop a plan for what she was calling "The Lenny Project." Liz liked Laurie Willis. She was the kind of caring police officer she could relate to, and she wanted to get to know more about her.

Liz showed up early at Police Headquarters, located in City Hall, expecting to have to wait until Laurie arrived, but when Liz looked up after giving her card to the receptionist, there came Laurie wheeling herself down the hallway in her direction.

City Hall was a newer building than those found in most older cities, but the inside of the Police Headquarters next door was like most she had seen in her career; a large 'bullpen' with multiple desks, and small offices along one wall, with some interrogation rooms.

Laurie wheeled up to Liz and gave her a hearty handshake, "I see you're an early bird as well, Liz."

"Maybe not on my days off. I can sleep all day when I get the chance. But when I have a troubling case on my mind, I just can't clear my mind to really relax," Liz replied.

"Well, this is certainly one of those," Laurie said. "Come on down to my office so we can decide how to approach this one."

Liz followed Laurie to her office and took a seat across from Laurie. Liz was impressed that the Department had made Laurie's office very wheelchair accessible, even providing her with a desk that allowed Laurie to wheel under it and have desk space and files which let her work easily.

"I see you noticed the amenities they've provided," Laurie said. "I tease the Chief that it's his way of hitting on me, which makes him blush. But actually, I know he feels responsible for me getting shot. My partner was appearing in court that day and my backup didn't show up during the drug bust. So, I ignored the procedures and entered the house alone. I should have waited, but I thought it was just a bunch of kids, and I could handle the situation. Their supplier was there and he's the one that shot me. He ran, but we found him the next day after one of the kids gave us his name."

"Darn! How long ago did this happen?" Liz asked.

"Six years ago. I was hospitalized for several months, and they attempted surgery to get my legs back, but the damage to the spinal cord was too severe."

"But you're back to work? That seems unusual. What does your family think of you coming back?"

"I was engaged to a great guy before this occurred. He wanted me to leave police work behind and have kids when we got married. And I was seriously considering asking the Chief for an off-street position that still allowed me to stay with the Department. I just hadn't mentioned the conversation yet with the Chief. My guy was devastated after the shooting. He's still with me, but we never married."

"I think that's why my guy is so worried. I met Steve during a bust of a trafficking operation while I was a state cop in Kentucky. After a couple close calls, I went to Law School and promised Steve I'd quit doing police work and undercover stuff in particular. Steve got to see the risks first-hand, and he lives in fear about the possible consequences. I just have a hard time letting the perps go free because we don't want to put these young girls on the stand in a trial."

"That's how I felt about these kids supplying drugs to other young teens. You see how that turned out for me, so your Steve's concerns are well founded," Laurie said.

"But your guy stayed with you. I guess that he's not a cop?" Liz asked.

"No. Felix is a Purchasing Agent at the shipyard here in Erie."

"You're kidding! Steve works at the shipyard. He's a naval architect. I'm sure that Felix and Steve must know one another. We need to get the four of us together."

"Think about it, Liz. Meeting me will prove to Steve that he is right."

"I'll need to take that chance, I guess. I want you and I to become friends."

"I certainly agree with that sentiment. We can discuss that later. But for now, what do we do about Lenny Simpson? I've checked him out and other than a minor scrape a couple years ago where he was caught stealing a pack of cigarettes at a gas station, he has a clean record. Both of his parents worked in the past, but his dad was laid off from the G.E. plant over a year ago. His mother works at a small manufacturer, assembling small parts for the auto industry. With his dad on unemployment and his mom's limited income, I can imagine their family finances are tight. I don't see any divorce in the files, but I'm not sure if the parents are still together. Divorces cost money, so they might have just split."

"Does Lenny have any siblings?" Liz asked.

"None living at home. He has an older sister, nineteen, but she lives with a guy over in Cleveland. Lenny supposedly lives with his parents in an apartment near the high school, and he's in ninth grade, per school records. He'll be going to high school next year."

"Okay, Laurie. After you asked me if Lenny knew I had been undercover at the modeling agency, I think I saw what you were thinking. By now, Lenny knows that Majestic Modeling and Rudy Radovich are gone. I could contact Lenny because I'm now out of work, asking him what he knows."

"That's what I was thinking," Laurie said. "But remember, we need to be careful not to be accused of entrapment. When I take him in for interrogation, I don't want him saying that you suggested criminal activity."

"Understood," Liz replied. "If necessary, I could wear a recorder to play back to Lenny in case he tries to say that. I have a guy who can do the recording for me."

"Alright. Keep your meeting low-key. Let him do the talking. Once you hear what he knows, we'll get back together," Laurie said.

Liz checked in at the D.A.'s office that same day and

told Mr. Pierson that she planned to meet Lenny outside the Middle School that afternoon. School had just started that week, following the summer break. She still had Burt's recording equipment at home and called Burt to ask his permission to use it. She said she didn't need his help because she could just carry the recorder.

Liz was standing on the opposite side of the street from the school and thought she had missed Lenny. The school sidewalk was nearly empty when Lenny came out. Liz watched him come out to the street and when he was about to turn down the sidewalk, Liz yelled out to him, "Lenny. Is that you?"

Lenny turned, and when he saw Liz, he smiled and waved.

"Can we talk, Lenny?" Liz then shouted.

"Lenny looked again and then crossed the street. "You're the model who was taking care of Rudy's shop, right? I don't remember your name?"

"It's Liz. How are you doing, Lenny? I just saw you those couple of times at Majestic."

"Well, you know that Rudy has disappeared, right?" Lenny said.

"Yeah. I showed up for work one morning and Rudy never came in. I came back the next day and found a big chain and lock on both doors. Rudy never called me."

"I heard he got in trouble because of the girls. A couple of them freaked out at a client's place, he told me. That's why I brought Linda to see him that day, but he wasn't there. Remember?"

"What do you mean, they freaked out? What happened?" Liz asked.

"Rudy told me he always asked the clients to start gentle with the young girls. Some of those guys wanted the girls to take their clothes off, but Rudy told them not to rush into sex. Some of those girls were virgins and had to be introduced slowly, you know?"

"Was that Rudy's intention for the young ones? I thought those girls were just models," Liz continued probing.

"There's not much money in modeling. At least that's what Rudy used to say. So he said he needed to get them sold for sexual favors as soon as possible."

"How much was Rudy paying you to bring those girls to him, Lenny?"

"It started out at $50, but once I started finding him young, but experienced girls, he was paying me $150. Rudy told me I should just break them in myself, but I don't want them getting me in trouble, so I stick with the older girls."

"Oh, I see. Like Lexy and Beth? They're older, right?" Liz asked.

"Wait, how do you know about Lexy and Beth?" Lenny asked Liz, looking at her curiously.

"Rudy mentioned them to me when I worked there."

Lenny seemed satisfied with Liz's answer and continued. "Those two were really hot. They told Rudy they'd do whatever was needed to make good money. Lexy liked me and showed me a good time, but Beth wasn't as friendly."

"I heard about a young Indian girl," Liz said. "Whatever happened to her?"

"I think she was one of the ones who freaked out. I remember Rudy telling me not to send him any more of those little prudes. He said he had to send her away to get her straightened out."

"Send her away? What would her parents have said to that?" Liz asked.

"I didn't get involved once I brought the girls to see Rudy. I don't know," Lenny answered.

"But what happened to Tiffany? She was one of the older ones, wasn't she?"

"I'm not sure how Rudy found Tiffany. I met her at school, and she seemed to like working for Rudy. I think she had problems at home and decided to end it all. Stupid! She had a good career ahead of her at Majestic."

Liz figured that Lenny was lying about Tiffany, knowing she had committed suicide, and he didn't want to be connected to her. But Liz started to think she had better stop. Lenny knew what he was doing, even using some of the older girls himself. It was time to let Laurie take over. Lenny didn't seem to understand the emotional damage he was causing these girls.

"So, Lenny. What are you doing now that Rudy has disappeared?" Liz asked.

"I'm trying to contact the guy in Ohio, but he's not answering his phone. I keep getting weird voice messages, like an answering machine. I have some other girls looking for some extra money, but I don't know what to do with them."

"Aren't you worried that these young girls might get hurt?

Some of the men Rudy was working with got a little rough," Liz said.

"Nah, they need to learn sooner or later. My sister has had two abortions already. She's doing okay. Life is tough. These girls should know that by now," Lenny responded.

"Well, Lenny, I've got to get moving. I guess you live with your mom and dad?" Liz asked.

"Just my dad," Lenny said. "My mom left us a couple years ago. Not sure where she is now."

"I'm sorry about that. It must be tough just to have your dad."

"Mom wasn't much of a mother. Dad said we're better off without her."

"Oh, I see. Maybe I'll see you around. Take care, Lenny."

"Yeah, Liz. See ya. If you find anyone looking for some nice talent, let me know. After Rudy and Eddie disappeared, all my customers are gone."

Liz was quite shocked by Lenny's attitude. But she also understood where the boy was coming from. He lacked a structured home life, and it appeared that his mother had tainted his attitude about women, and his father very well could be the source of Lenny's disregard for females in general. Liz wondered if any amount of counseling would change Lenny's outlook on life. Laurie Willis was surely going to have her hands full with this one.

Liz called Laurie and summarized the conversation she had just had with Lenny. "Was Lenny aware that any of the girls were being used for illicit sexual purposes?" Laurie asked Liz.

"He certainly was aware," Liz replied. "He said that Rudy

Radovich had told him that there wasn't much money to be made in modeling, so he needed to get them sold for sexual favors as soon as possible. I know that he was aware of the Jandra girl because Rudy told Lenny not to send him any more of those little prudes. Lenny even admitted that Rudy had to send her away 'to get her straightened out,' as he put it."

"What about Tiffany, the girl who committed suicide?" Laurie asked.

"Lenny said he didn't know where Rudy had found Tiffany, though I suspect he's lying. It looks like he knew about Lexy and Beth. Lexy was even offering herself to Lenny, though I'm not sure if Lenny is the one who brought those girls to Rudy. It almost sounded like they went to Rudy on their own. From what we learned during the raid on that Ohio motel, those two girls had a terrible home life and knew what they were getting into. They just became upset because of the rough sex, which Rudy had told them wouldn't happen."

"We have a real mess on our hands here, Liz. That's for sure. You've given me enough to know that we have cause to bring Lenny in for questioning. It doesn't sound like we'll have any parental support or guidance, and Lenny is too old to get many benefits from a Foster Home. I have a great counselor in mind, Roberto Arroyo, who will work with Lenny, but this boy may be too hardened to respond. I know Roberto will do his best. That's all we can hope for."

"Okay, Laurie. Keep me informed, and let me know if you need my help. I recorded my conversation with Lenny if you need it. I'll put together a written case report about my meeting. And by the way, I found out from Lenny that his mother left the family quite a while ago. It's only his father and him. His sister is nineteen and lives in Cleveland, I think you said."

"Thanks, Liz. Let's talk about getting together socially. Our goal will be to keep Steve and Felix from talking about the shipyard."

"You got that right," Liz replied.

18

Laurie Meets Lenny

Laurie Willis had Lenny Simpson brought into her office on a juvenile warrant for questioning concerning the Majestic Modeling case. She also contacted Lenny's father and requested that he be in attendance during the questioning. Leonard Simpson Sr. wanted to know if his son, Lenny, needed an attorney. Laurie told Mr. Simpson that there was no evidence that Lenny had committed a crime, but they could have a lawyer in attendance during the questioning if he desired.

Leonard Simpson and his son came into Laurie's office the next morning. Laurie asked Mr. Simpson if they had contacted an attorney and Mr. Simpson replied, "Lenny told me he hadn't done anything wrong, so why would we waste money on a lawyer?"

Laurie began with the typical name, address, relatives, schooling, and other biographical information, and then started asking questions about the case.

"Lenny, do you know Elisa Jandra?"

Lenny answered, "Yes. She goes to my school."

"How old is Elisa, Lenny?"

"I have no idea," Lenny said curtly.

"Is she in your grade at school? Older? Younger?"

"She's younger," Lenny said, again very rudely.

"How much behind you, Lenny? One grade? Two?"

"I think three grades, but I'm not sure," Lenny answered.

At this point, Lenny's father asked, "What are these questions all about? This seems like a waste of our time."

"I'm getting there, Mr. Simpson. Let me continue," Laurie said calmly.

"And Lenny, what about Tiffany Edmunds? Do you know her?"

"She's dead. Don't you read the news?" Lenny said, almost sneering.

"Wait! Are you insinuating that Lenny had something to do with some dead girl?" Mr. Simpson questioned, with revulsion in his tone.

"Tiffany's death was ruled a suicide, Mr. Simpson. I just want to know if Lenny knew her. And what grade was Tiffany in, Lenny?" Laurie continued.

"I think she was in my class," Lenny answered.

"So, if you are sixteen, can I assume that Tiffany was sixteen?"

"I guess. How would I know if maybe she flunked a grade?" Lenny answered.

"Well, I guess she hadn't flunked a grade, Lenny. In fact, Tiffany would not have turned sixteen until this month,"

Laurie said. "Now, let me change the subject a little. Do you know a man named Rudy Radovich?"

"I've heard that name, I guess," Lenny said.

"Did you work for Mr. Radovich?" Laurie asked.

"Hell no! What would I do, working at a modeling place?" Lenny said.

"You seem to know what Mr. Radovich's business was. Are you sure you never did any work for him?" Laurie continued.

Again, Mr. Simpson jumped in, "Just what is all this about? Lenny is a Middle School student. What is this working thing all about?"

"We're almost to that point, Mr. Simpson. Then I think you'll understand," Laurie answered.

"So, Lenny. We have all of Mr. Radovich's files and we have found numerous payments made to you over the last two years. Rudy liked details, so he entered the following notations:

'Elisa Jandra – 13, $150.00 - Lenny' and then
'Tiffany Edmunds – 15, $175.00 - Lenny'.

We found eight other such entries, totaling just over $1400.00. What work were you doing for Mr. Radovich, Lenny?"

Now Mr. Simpson became interested, and he asked Lenny, "Christ, Lenny! What the hell were you doing? That's serious money."

"Just running errands, Dad," Lenny replied, looking more sheepish than before.

"Running errands, Lenny?" Laurie asked. "We understand

that you were acting like a talent scout for Mr. Radovich. He paid you to bring young girls to his studio. Isn't that true, Lenny?"

"A few times. If girls at school wanted to become models, I'd suggest going to Majestic."

"Here's another person, Lenny. Do you know Eddie Silvers?"

"Doesn't ring a bell," Lenny said.

"Well, I've spoken to two young women, Lexy, and Beth, who are runaways from your school. They told me that you've visited them over in Ohio, at the brothel that is run by Eddie Silvers. Eddie worked for Rudy Radovich as well, managing that brothel. That is where Elisa Jandra was held against her will, being sold for sex, after she was raped by one of Rudy's clients. Are you telling me that you were not aware of any of this, Lenny?"

Mr. Simpson spoke again, "Lenny, I want to hear an answer to her question. Just how involved have you been in this business? After your sister's problems, why would you do this?"

"Dad, I didn't do anything wrong! Don't blame me for what Rudy did with those girls?"

"Miss Willis, my daughter was a runaway and she had two abortions before she was age-eighteen. I'm sorry for my tone earlier. I thought Lenny would have learned from his sister's life, just how serious things can be for a young girl away from home. It tore my family apart, and I guess I ignored Lenny because he's a boy. Now it appears that he's sold these young girls into the same life that his sister has lived. I assume that Lenny will need to answer for all of this?"

"Mr. Simpson, I'm glad to see that you understand. As morally culpable as Lenny may be, I haven't found any evidence that he has broken any laws. I do think he needs counseling, and I hope you will agree. The Edmunds family is not aware of the circumstances that led to their daughter's suicide, so we do not want to interfere with their grief. Tiffany was brought to Majestic, allegedly by Lenny, and the modeling went from topless to nude, finally leading to her being raped. Apparently, she was no longer able to deal with the situation, and she took her own life.

"However, Elisa Jandra is still traumatized and physically damaged by multiple rapes. She is also overcoming the drug addiction her captors caused. If the Jandra family needs help, I'm hoping that Lenny can eventually meet her parents and ask for forgiveness. I cannot demand that, but I'm hoping that Lenny will eventually understand how the trafficking of these girls for sex has damaged them for life. My purpose today was to show both of you that Lenny has to change."

"What would you recommend, Miss Willis? I want Lenny to take responsibility for his actions and I'll agree with anything you recommend," Lenny's father said. "I know this is also my fault for not being a good father. I was upset with life after our family broke up, and I'm sorry to say that I ignored Lenny's activities. I should have known from my daughter's experiences that just putting a roof over his head was not enough."

"If you agree, Mr. Simpson, I'd like Lenny to attend

counseling sessions here at the courthouse. Mr. Roberto Arroyo is a very serious, experienced counselor. I think that he and Lenny could work well together. I can arrange for you and your son to meet with Roberto, and then you can decide. I also need to inform you that Lenny will be on our Juvenile Offender's Watch List. It doesn't mean that Lenny is on probation because he hasn't actually broken any laws, but I think you will agree that Lenny has the potential to be led into criminal activity. Therefore, we will have Mr. Arroyo provide weekly progress reports to my office. Can you understand my concerns, Mr. Simpson?"

"I certainly understand, Miss Willis. And might I ask that you also keep me informed of Lenny's progress with Mr. Arroyo, and any concerns you may have?" Mr. Simpson asked.

"I'll let you arrange communications with Mr. Arroyo, but I will certainly let you know if I have any concerns. Thank you for your cooperation, Mr. Simpson."

"Thank you, Miss Willis. As I said, this is my fault, as well as Lenny's."

With that decided, Laurie picked up her phone and called Roberto Arroyo. She briefly described the purpose of her call and asked if Roberto had time for a short meeting, to arrange for sessions with Lenny and his father. Roberto asked Laurie to send Lenny and Mr. Simpson down the hall to his office in the courthouse, which was adjacent to the police station.

Roberto Arroyo was 44 years old and married with three children; two daughters, sixteen and twelve, and a son, aged fourteen. He had been a local sports hero in high school, playing football and baseball. He was accepted to college on a football scholarship and blew out a knee in his freshman year. Discouraged, he tried to join the military, but his knee condition ruined that attempt as well. So, Roberto decided to take his studies seriously after that, and his degree in psychology got him started as a high school counselor, back at his alma mater. When he saw the growing problem with teens dabbling with crime and being arrested while still in high school, Roberto obtained a master's degree in Juvenile Correctional Counseling. He offered his services to the Erie Police Department, and eventually took a full-time position with the County.

When Lenny and his father entered his office, Roberto rose, shook hands with both of them, and invited them to take a seat. Knowing that Mr. Simpson had agreed to counseling, Roberto directed his attention to Lenny. "So, tell me, Lenny, how may I help you?" he asked.

Lenny seemed surprised by the question. "What do you mean? That lady told us to come over here," he said.

"If you're forced to attend meetings with me, Lenny, what good will come from that? Do you see any need to talk to me? If not, maybe we're both wasting our time," Roberto answered.

"I guess my dad thinks I need help," Lenny said.

"The real question is, do you think you need help, Lenny?"

"The lady said that I didn't do anything wrong. So, I'm not sure why I'm here," Lenny said.

"From what I heard, Miss Willis said she couldn't find that you had committed any crimes. Doing something wrong is a totally different matter, don't you think?" Roberto countered.

"I don't understand," Lenny said.

"From what I understand, you brought some young girls to see a man, and that man led them into pornography, and then into forced sex. You were paid to bring him these girls. What do you think he had planned for them, Lenny?"

"I didn't ask, I guess," Lenny said.

"You seem to be a smart young man, Lenny. You must have suspected what that man had planned for them. Look at it this way: if you give a box of matches to a small child, and they get burned, or even burn their house down, would you be responsible for what happened to them?"

"That's different. The little kid doesn't know what matches can do," Lenny said.

"I'm not sure if it is very different, Lenny. These young girls were looking for some extra money, thinking it was just modeling for pictures. Did they know about the nude photos and the sex before you brought them to that place?"

Lenny seemed rattled when he said, "They should have figured that out. They could have said no if they didn't want to do it."

"You don't really believe that, do you? Look at where you are right now, Lenny. You're sitting in my office because Miss Willis and your father want you to be here. You feel uncomfortable, but you don't just walk out. Think of those girls posing for some older man. When he told them to take off their clothes, because it was part of the job, they did it because someone older than them, an adult they thought they could trust, told them it was okay. They were told it was a required part of the job. Didn't that all occur because you never told those girls what you really suspected was actually going to happen?"

Lenny seemed speechless, but Lenny's father said, "Thank you, Mr. Arroyo. I understand, and now I believe that Lenny also understands. How often would you like to see Lenny? I'd be happy to get him here whenever you want him."

"Can we start with three times a week? Then we can see how things are going and adjust the schedule as needed."

19

District Attorney's Office

Burt arrived at the D.A.'s office to speak to Tom Pierson and Liz Trent about his experience at the hotel bar. Liz and Tom were waiting for him in Tom Pierson's office when he arrived.

Liz rose and shook Burt's hand when he entered. "No hugging, Burt. I don't want Mr. Pierson to get the wrong idea."

Tom Pierson laughed. "Liz has been telling me about all the efforts you made to keep her safe during this whole Majestic investigation. Particularly the sting with Liz in that customer's home."

"I just got the feeling that this young woman was worth protecting, Tom. And after meeting her young man, Steve, I took that responsibility even more seriously."

"Yes. Steve sure thinks the world of you, Burt," said Tom.

"So, tell me. What has happened with those pedophiles who were taking those little kids from that so-called daycare center, and the guy who Liz found with all those pictures of the little girls?"

"Most of them will only get probation because we cannot prove that they abused the girls. But at least they're listed as potential sex offenders. The man that you and Liz busted, as well as a few others who kept pictures of the kids, have been charged with child pornography. Those cases are going to be tried, and I hope the photos will lead to convictions," Pierson answered.

"It would have been great to get them for sexual relations with a minor," Liz said, "but they had high-priced lawyers that argued they were using willing kids for artistic pursuits. Real BS, but most of them will win with that argument."

"And I assume that Radovich will be put away for a long time," Burt said.

"Yes. We have more than enough evidence against him. We've had to keep him in solitary at the County Lock-up because the guards overheard the other prisoners planning to beat him up."

"Too bad they overheard the plans, I think," Burt said.

"No comment," Tom said. "But what's this about a business card, which involves another trafficking scheme?"

"Well, as you know, there's always a new trafficker lurking around and ready to pick up the business when the previous one gets caught. I don't know if this guy is new, but he knows that Radovich's clients are looking for a new supplier. I happened to be talking with a bartender at one of the waterfront hotels, and he informed me of a young man who's been coming into the bar and talking to all the lone men he finds in there. He'd come in several times a week and will nurse one drink while he walks around chatting up the single guys. Fred said he would often see him hand out business cards to these men as he worked the room."

"What made you suspect that this involved trafficking, Burt?" Tom Pierson asked.

"Again, it was the bartender who first suspected it. He knew Hendrickson's reputation with the 20-something women, but he overheard the other man telling Hendrickson that Majestic was shut down, and then he overheard him asking, 'How young are you looking for?'"

"What did Hendrickson say?" Liz asked, her interest peaking.

"The guy noticed Fred's head turn, so he pulled Hendrickson over to a table away from the bar. But that question bothered Fred so much that he remembered it, especially since he had heard about Majestic being in the 'young girl trade.'"

"So, you got this card from the bartender?" Pierson asked.

"No. It gets better. Fred told me the guy hadn't been in lately, but he suspected he'd drop by that evening. I stuck around for dinner, and, sure enough, the guy walked in at the time Fred suspected he would. Fred signaled to me when the guy arrived and, true to what Fred had told me, this guy soon began to make the rounds. He was about to leave when he noticed me sitting alone and walked over to me. He was careful with his approach at first, but eventually asked me if I was, 'looking for an experienced woman or someone younger?'"

"He actually asked about age?" Liz said, obviously getting upset.

"He sure did," Burt said, "he even went further to say he knew somebody, 'with a houseful of girls, twelve to thirty.' He said they were all Russians, willing to please."

"This certainly sounds like a new operation," Pierson said. "Other than the two young, Eastern European kids we found at the 'day care' place, and some pictures that Liz found at Majestic, it didn't appear that Radovich dealt with European traffickers. But he possibly got some of his European kids from this guy."

"That was my gut feeling as well. If you want me to call the guy for more information, I'd be happy to help," Burt said.

Liz picked the card up off the desk and said, "Not very descriptive, is it? 'ENTERTAINMENT? CALL 814-555-7399'"

"Look at your phone keypad, Liz. I may be wrong, but '7399' could stand for 'SEXY.'"

"Damn! You're right. I bet that's it," Liz said after typing the numbers into her phone.

"I'll run this new information through channels and see if law enforcement has any information, or possibly an ongoing investigation. As the D.A., I cannot initiate a new investigation. The Majestic situation was part of an existing, local complaint, you understand?"

"I hate to admit this, but I was one of those people who had heard about human trafficking but assumed that it only happened in foreign countries, or cities like New York and Detroit, not right here where I live. Now that I'm aware of the problem, I can't turn away from it. I feel like I need to do more to stop it," Burt said.

"Burt, can you please share that feeling with Steve? He thinks I'm crazy," Liz said.

"It's not that Steve isn't concerned, Liz. He's just more concerned about your safety. He thought you were going to fight the traffickers in the courtroom, not continue to be on the front lines. He loves you and doesn't want to lose you. Don't be too rough on him!"

"Yeah. I promised him I would leave the undercover stuff behind. But now you know how hard it is to do that, once you see the damage it does to these kids, firsthand."

"I guess we'll need to do a better job of explaining this to Steve. Maybe I can help," Burt said.

Tom Pierson, who had been listening to Liz and Burt's exchange, added that he didn't want Liz to be doing any more undercover work, like the one she had done at Majestic. Now that she was known to be part of the D.A.'s office, Tom thought the traffickers would know who she is, and that her cover would be blown for any future undercover operations.

"From here forward, Liz will be much more valuable for her experience, and she can work with other investigators and with the victims. Her first-hand experience will be invaluable."

"I think Steve will be happy to hear that," Burt said. "I feel for that guy!"

Liz looked from Tom to Burt. She knew Tom was right, but she still hoped there would be some undercover work in her future, even if not in the immediate future. She was okay with that...for now.

20

Lenny

Lenny's father made sure that Lenny was attending his 3-day-a-week sessions with Roberto Arroyo. Roberto had an instinctive talent when it came to communicating with teens. He seldom addressed their failings, but instead tried to find their interests and dreams. Roberto waited for the time when his troubled 'projects', as he called them, would start to ask questions. Those questions usually led to what was troubling them, the root cause of their character flaws.

In Lenny's case, his big concern was his sister, Debbie. They had been very close as young children because their parents were constantly squabbling about money, long hours, and so on. They weren't abusing the children in any way, but they were ignoring them, so the siblings became very dependent on one another.

Debbie had a rebellious childhood that climaxed following their parents' separation. His sister loved their mother, but then their mother left. Their father worked two jobs and was seldom home, so Debbie sought love on the streets. She became pregnant at fourteen and had an abortion. Mr. Simpson tried his best, but certainly, he did not understand his daughter's problems. He called her a "loose woman, like her mother," setting off a chain of rebellious actions that drove his daughter even further away from home. This time, she had been gone for over a year, and no one knew where she was. At sixteen, she returned home, pregnant again and strung out on drugs. The boy who Debbie thought loved her, had asked her to sleep with his friends, and she did so to please him. When she found out that those friends were paying the boyfriend for those sessions, she finally realized he was pimping her, and not really in love with her.

Mr. Simpson sought counseling for Debbie, but because Lenny was a boy, he assumed that Lenny was fine.

Lenny was still young, so when his sister became pregnant, he didn't understand that she had been sold for sex during the time she disappeared. She aborted the second pregnancy too and ended up staying at home long enough to finish high school. But the moment she graduated, she moved to Cleveland where she was living with a guy in his parents' house.

When things seemed comfortable enough between himself and Lenny, Roberto invited Lenny over to have a barbeque dinner with his family. So, one Saturday, Lenny joined Roberto and his son in their backyard where the three of them played catch. Lenny had never played catch with his father, and none of his friends were into baseball. He felt uncomfortable at first, but he enjoyed watching them joking together, and the banter between Roberto and his son.

During dinner, Roberto's eldest daughter, who was planning for her Junior Prom, asked her parents if they wanted to meet the young man who had invited her to the dance. Lenny thought that request of her parents was strange, neither of his own parents had ever questioned his activities. However, his biggest shock was that Roberto and his wife treated their youngest daughter like a child, not at all the way Lenny was used to thinking about girls.

He mentioned that during his next meeting with Roberto. "Mr. Arroyo," he began, "when will you stop treating your daughters like kids?"

Roberto glanced up from his notepad, a little taken aback. "What do you mean, Lenny?"

"Well, I think my sister was having sex around twelve or thirteen and had her first abortion at fourteen. Yet your sixteen-year-old has to ask you if you want to meet the guy who's taking her to the prom. And your younger daughter probably still plays with dolls. Are you telling me that those things are normal?"

Roberto smiled and leaned back in his chair, studying Lenny. The poor boy had already seen more than any boy his age should ever have to see, so he was not surprised that in Lenny's mind, Roberto's family life was outside of the norm.

"I suppose every family sets their own standards, Lenny. But let me ask you this, do you think that your sister is happy? Does she visit you and your dad?"

"Debbie never comes home. I visited her last year in Cleveland. She works long hours and the guy she's with is a bum. So no, I don't think she's very happy."

"Listen, Lenny, I'm really sorry that you didn't have your mom around when you were young. I think your dad is a nice guy, but working two jobs and trying to raise two young kids had to have been tough. Your sister would have been happier if she could have stayed home, but she was starved for affection. Finding that affection from false people, who really didn't care about her, has ruined her life, don't you think?"

"Yeah. Probably," Lenny answered.

"So, to answer your first question, I'm trying hard to protect my kids from bad influences. I want to meet her date for the Prom and if I don't like him, I might decide to tell her she can't go. However, I've also learned to trust my daughter's judgment, so I doubt she would have accepted an invitation from someone I wouldn't like. Like my wife and I, I guess she has also set high standards for her boyfriends."

"And what about the younger daughter? Does she spend time together with guys?"

"Not at all before high school. And just like her older sister, we will monitor her relationships carefully."

"And your son? He's about my age. Is he dating yet?"

"No. I know he is attracted to some of the girls in his class. He told me he was, and I started talking to him about respect. A boy needs to know the long-term damage done to a girl who is abused. Not just physical damage, but emotional damage as well. That is a boy's responsibility, not to cross that line, especially with very young girls. The girl may feel attraction to the boy and even say she wants to be intimate, but afterwards, she will regret it. I know that it's a tough age, feeling sexual attraction, but somehow, respect has to take place and avoid the regrets that would follow."

Lenny then said, "I saw Elisa Jandra at school today. She's moving to a different, private school. When I saw her, she looked a lot like your youngest daughter. Elisa was thirteen when I took her to meet Rudy. He said she'd only be used for modeling, but now that I hear what happened to her, and afterward put her in that hotel in Ohio, I think I know Rudy lied to me. I went to visit Lexy out there and was surprised to see Elisa. They had her so drugged up, that she didn't recognize me when I talked to her. I asked Eddie about that and he said that she kept screaming when she was with the clients, so they had to drug her to shut her up. That really bothered me."

Roberto said, "So, you can see that my daughter is no different from Elisa Jandra. Elisa wanted some extra money, but now she may spend the rest of her life in therapy."

"Why aren't you telling me what a terrible person I am, Roberto? I ruined Elisa's life."

"You made a terrible mistake, Lenny, but you aren't a terrible person. The fact that you now can see how troubled Elisa will be, shows me that you care. Maybe if your father wasn't so worried about his and your sister's problems, he should have taught you about respecting others. That didn't happen, so what do you think should happen now?"

"Can I help Elisa somehow? I didn't mean to do this to her. I thought she knew what was happening, but now I understand that she didn't know."

"I can ask Miss Willis what she thinks, but first, I think

you need to talk to Miss Willis and ask her what to do. We don't want to add more stress to Elisa's life," Roberto said.

"I also want to tell you about Tiffany. I did bring her to meet Rudy. Tiffany liked me but I was more interested in Lexy. I really thought that Tiffany was old enough to stay out of trouble. She was almost sixteen, and I thought she was experienced," Lenny said.

"What do you mean by experienced?" Roberto asked though he was sure of what Lenny implied.

"I guess I thought that she had slept with some of the guys in my class, But I've been asking my friends at school about it now, and they told me that they thought Tiffany was still a virgin. They thought I knew that."

"Why did you think otherwise, Lenny?"

"Probably because my sister was sleeping with guys when she was real young. I thought all girls did that, I guess."

"Lenny, that is not normal behavior, and as you now see, it leads to other problems. So, what made you want to talk about Tiffany?"

"One of the girls at school said that Tiffany talked to her about having sex for the first time with an older man. That was about a week before her suicide. The girl feels bad now because she says she asked Tiffany if Tiffany was a whore. She thinks that hurt Tiffany's feelings. When Tiffany killed herself just a few days later, the girl felt terrible about what she'd said and wondered if her words pushed Tiffany to do what she did.

"That's a tough question, Lenny. I wish Tiffany could have asked for help from a counselor, which might have prevented her from reaching that point. She must have felt like she couldn't ask her parents for advice, which is too bad."

"I know that Tiffany wasn't happy with the nude photos. She told me that, but she also told me that she didn't want to give up the money. I told her she had to do what the guys asked, or she'd be washed up. I wish I hadn't said that to her."

"I'm impressed with how your attitude has changed, Lenny. You now see how important it is to think about people with respect and you understand the consequences of what you say, as well as what you fail to say. If you carry that attitude for the rest of your life, you will become a good man. Maybe you can offer your experiences to young people at school, to keep them from making bad decisions."

"I wish I could have met you before, Roberto. I feel very guilty about some of the things I've done."

"We can't change those now, Lenny. Look to the future and do what you now know is right and help others. That's the best any of us can do."

A few days later, Liz called Laurie Willis, agitated. "Have you talked to Lenny Simpson since our meeting?"

"No, but Roberto has sent me a couple written reports. He says he's quite happy and even surprised by Lenny's progress. Why do you ask?"

"I just got a call from Mrs. Jandra. Lenny showed up at her home today."

"Oh, my God. Roberto said that Lenny asked about helping Elisa, but Roberto told Lenny that Elisa seeing Lenny might just upset her. Apparently, Lenny found out that Elisa was changing schools, which made him feel very guilty."

"Well, Mrs. Jandra said that Lenny showed up mid-morning, knowing that Elisa would not be at home. Lenny apparently had skipped school, and he stood at her door, started to apologize, and then broke into sobs. Mrs. Jandra invited him inside and Lenny told her how sorry he was for taking her daughter to Majestic Modeling. He said he now understood that Elisa was a nice girl, not like the others he knew that worked for Radovich. Lenny told Mrs. Jandra that he was responsible for everything that happened to her daughter, and he knew she could never forgive him, but he wanted her to know that he was sorry."

"I'm not sure what to think," Laurie said. "I'm glad to see that Lenny now understands what he did, but I'm sorry that he upset Mrs. Jandra."

"That's what I first thought," Liz said. "But Mrs. Jandra said that seeing Lenny's emotional outburst has helped her. She thought none of the guilty parties cared about what they had done to her daughter but seeing Lenny's repentance helped to heal her hatred. And knowing that Radovich will be in prison for a long time, she is hoping that their family can start to heal. Her one open question is whether or not to tell Elisa about Lenny's visit."

"I'm happy that Lenny didn't try to contact Elisa. It appears that the timing of his appearance was intentional, to avoid seeing Elisa. I'll let Roberto know about this development, and I'll also ask him to speak with Elisa's counselor, so they can discuss the situation. How does that sound, Liz?"

"I think that would be best. Thanks, Laurie."

"By the way, one thing bothers me about what you said.

Lenny told Mrs. Jandra that Elisa wasn't like the others he knew that worked for Radovich. What girls was he comparing her to?"

"I assume he was referring to Lexy and Beth, and maybe including his own sister, though she didn't work at Majestic. Lexy and Beth were two 16-year-old runaways who went to Radovich willingly. In fact, Lenny was having sex with one of them out at the motel in Ohio. Both of those girls came from dysfunctional homes where they were being abused. In fact, Beth's mother told her to leave home before her father killed her someday."

"I know that motel was raided and closed down. What happened to those two girls?" Laurie asked.

"We referred them to a group home here in Erie. I must admit, I haven't checked up on them since that time," Liz answered.

"I'm going to ask Roberto about them as well. Kids from abusive homes tend to stay in *'the life'* as it's called. As bad as it may sound to us, being sold for sex, their handlers, pimps if you prefer, actually treat them better than they were treated at home. Many of them are sexually abused by their parents, so sex is not a deterrent, particularly with younger men. I'm hoping that the group home is not considering sending them to a foster home, because many of the homes that accept older kids like that, turn out to be emotional, if not physically abusive as well. The girls would just run away again, and they might never survive."

"Understood, Laurie. According to Burt Snyder, Lexy

seemed willing to leave that motel once she knew it was being shut down. She just didn't want to go home."

"This marketing of children has reached epidemic proportions in this country. Just look at what we've found in our community: runaway teens, selling pre-teens for nude modeling, and importing kids from overseas for pedophile use. We can't keep up with the traffickers, as a new one takes over as soon as we close one down."

"Does Erie have a program for rescued, sex-trafficked kids?" Liz asked.

"There is a Crime Victims Center that has a Sexual Assault Response Center. They deal with all forms of sexual assault, including incest, date rape, and assault on the streets. I'm not sure if they separate trafficking from the others."

"I think we need to look into that," Liz said. "Trafficked girls tend to return to their pimps, particularly if they have known abuse at home. They believe that physical pain is part of a loving relationship, as long as their pimp tells them he loves them and occasionally does something nice for them. Many times, just an apology for beating them is believed to be a sign that the pimp actually loves them."

"How is that even possible?" Laurie asked.

"Remember, Laurie. We have experienced real love. If someone beats us up, even just hits us, we understand that it isn't right. Many of these girls have never experienced real love, so they don't understand. Look at the difference between Lexy and Beth, versus Tiffany and Elisa. Lexy and Beth only experienced violence at home, so at the motel in Ohio, they felt safer than at home, despite being sold for sex. Even the false promises about being treated gently by their 'Johns' were a form of affection in their minds. Whereas Tiffany and Elisa came from loving families. Therefore, Tiffany couldn't deal with being used and took her own life. Elisa Jandra had to be drugged after she was raped the first time and still suffers trauma from those experiences. She would never want to go back to that life."

"What can we do about girls like Lexy and Beth? We can't just let them run back to that life. I assume they won't live long, being used many times each day. And of course, they could be killed by a beating. Will they ever decide that they need to return to a normal life, Liz?"

"What is normal life for them, Laurie? They've never experienced what we consider normal. I have a great book I'll loan you, *Girls Like Us*, written by Rachel Lloyd. Rachel came from a home life of abuse, As a young teen, she left home and was taken in by a man who sold her for sex, earning money to pay for his drug habit. That man sold her to another guy who continued selling her and beating her due to his mental issues. She finally ran away and went to school, earned a degree, and now runs the Girls Educational and Mentoring Services in New York. She specializes in slowly getting into these girls' heads, to convince them to stay off the streets and away from their pimps. She explains in her book that even after ten years away from her own pimp, after she was now successfully running her own service organization, she was still tempted to call him, thinking he might have changed as he got older. She even wrote his phone number down, but at the last minute, she knew she had to stop. She keeps that paper in her wallet so she can show 'her girls' how strong that urge is to go back to 'the life,' even after they realize how terrible it was."

"Oh my, Liz. Are we fighting a losing battle?"

"We can't think that way, Laurie. If we stop fighting, the perps win. At least we can save those we find and make it harder for the traffickers to recruit more girls."

"Are there specific things we can do?" Laurie asked.

"One important thing is to train our police and court systems," Liz continued. "Most cops look at prostitutes as being willing participants. They cannot believe that a sixteen or even a thirteen-year-old girl is being forced to solicit sex. If they saw Elisa Jandra screaming during rape, and being drugged for further repeated rapes, maybe they would understand. Or maybe if they saw the background of girls like Lexy and Beth, being abused at home, they might understand. Instead, they arrest the girl prostitutes, take the names of the 'Johns,' and warn them not to do that again. Unfortunately, the girl now has a record, and the 'Johns' just walk away. If the girl is dragged into court to testify against her pimp, she's afraid, and many judges are forced to dismiss the charges. The judge then remands the girl to some service for therapy. She will eventually run back to her pimp because her family has now disowned her, or they were the ones that started the abuse in the first place."

"I don't think I've ever thought of how these girls ended up in these places, and certainly never understood why they didn't just run away. They have nowhere to go, do they?" Laurie said.

"Most of the success stories are girls who survived, like

Rachel Lloyd, who now work in service organizations to help other trafficked girls. If they're passionate about wanting to change their pattern and can focus that passion on helping others, they usually succeed in turning away from that *life*."

"Then let's focus on Lexy and Beth. Maybe we can find a way to keep them from going back," Laurie said.

"I agree," Liz replied. "I have an idea. What if I ask Lexy and Beth to help Elisa Jandra recover from her trauma? We could ask Roberto and Jandra's therapist to be involved if Mr. and Mrs. Jandra agree. If the older girls see what has happened to Elisa, it could shock them into seeing that they need to stay away from that situation."

"That just might work," Laurie said. I'll talk to Roberto, and you can contact the Jandras. Sound like a plan?"

"Yes, I'm on it," Liz replied.

21

Liz - The China Solution

Liz volunteered to help the State Police Crisis Unit handle the young Chinese and Moldovan children they had rescued from the fake daycare center. The opinion of the State Police was that Hu Yang and Chu Hua Zhao, the two adults found caring for the children, should be deported to China. Despite Liz's telling Laura Griffin, the State's investigator, about her lengthy conversation with Hu Yang, the police were going to recommend deportation on the grounds of criminal activity.

Liz asked Tom Pierson for permission to plead her case directly to the INS, the Immigration and Naturalization Service, and Tom agreed. The nearest Field Office was in Pittsburgh, and Liz called. She eventually found a person familiar with the case, and the Agent agreed to visit Liz in Erie, as well as talk with the two Chinese adults.

Liz found that the young, fourteen-year-old boy from Moldova, whose name was Ivan, spoke quite good English, and she had spoken with him several times at length. He had been sexually abused during his time at the "daycare," but he somehow had dealt with the situation better than the Moldovan girl, who refused to speak and could not even make eye contact with anyone.

The boy said that his family had died back in Moldova, and he was begging on the streets when a man offered to take him to the United States. They traveled across Europe, and the man would arrange what he called 'sex adventures' with men along the way. When they reached Italy, the man got them aboard a ship, and the boy said that three weeks later, he was put in a small skiff and brought to shore. He thought they were in the United States, but he later learned it was Canada. There, he was put in the trunk of a car and told to be quiet. They crossed the border, and he came to the house where Mr. Rudy had him living. He saw money exchanged and he never saw that man from Moldova again.

Liz realized that that man had just used Ivan to finance his own trip to the United States and then just sold him off.

Liz asked Ivan about the Moldovan girl, but he said she was already at the house when he arrived. He thinks she was about ten when he arrived, but he had no idea how long she'd been there. He tried talking to her in their language, but she never answered. Then, maybe three weeks later, he heard a truck pull into the driveway early in the morning. He heard some noise and then the truck left. He then fell back to sleep. The next morning, he saw all the Chinese kids, huddled together downstairs. They all looked sick and skinny. Then he saw Hu and Chu Hua in the kitchen, trying to cook oatmeal, and they were making chopsticks out of old pieces of wood they found on the back porch.

Liz asked Ivan about the visits that were made, bringing him and the Chinese children to various places. Ivan said that Hu would always argue with Mr. Rudy about taking the children out, but he understood Mr. Rudy telling Hu that the children needed to earn money to become citizens, and then be adopted. Ivan said that even he understood that was not how it should be. Hu would always talk quietly to the children who were being taken to places, and Ivan wondered what he was telling them. Then one day, Hu asked Ivan if he understood English, and Ivan nodded. Hu told Ivan, "Be brave. I will find a way to stop this."

Liz asked Ivan, "What do you think Hu meant by saying that to you?"

"I asked Hu, 'Are you saying this to your girls?' and he said, 'Yes. This must stop. I do not know how. Sorry.'"

"So, Ivan, do you think Hu and Chu Hua are bad people?"

"No. I think they wanted to save their girls and the boy. Mr. Rudy is the bad person."

"Ivan, if I have you talk to a Government man, can you tell him what you just told me? They want to find good, safe homes for you and all the children, but they believe Hu and Chu Hua are bad people. Can you help me to tell them the truth?"

"Hu and Chu Hua are not bad. I can say this."

Liz met the INS agent, Willard Thomas at the D.A.'s office in Erie. Tom Pierson told Agent Thomas that he had agreed to let Liz Trent work with the State investigators at the home where the Chinese and Moldovan children were found because she had prior experience with such matters. Pierson then explained that the State Police charged the two adults and filed for deportation, also that the people at the Juvenile Social Services had moved the children to an Erie shelter for abused women. At the shelter, the Chinese children gathered in a corner, shuddering with fear, and refused to eat. The Moldovan girl would scream whenever someone came near her. Liz convinced the Social Services staff to return all the children to the home out near the New York border and to allow the two Chinese adults to care for them.

"But I understand that those adults were responsible for the abuse of those children. Why should they be allowed any freedom? They may try to escape," Agent Thomas said.

"We want you to meet them this afternoon, but first of all, Miss Trent would like you to meet one of the children. Liz brought young Ivan, the boy from Moldova to our office. He speaks good English, and he experienced what really happened to those Chinese children, and how Hu Yang acted and treated those children. I'll let Liz take over from here."

Liz took Agent Thomas into her office where they found Ivan playing games on Liz's iPad. Ivan stood up and smiled at Liz.

"Ivan, this is the Government man I told you about. His name is Mr. Thomas. Can we ask you a few questions about your life with the Chinese children?"

Ivan said, "Yes, Miss Liz. What can I tell you?"

After about 45 minutes of casual talk with Ivan, Agent

Thomas agreed to meet Mr. Yang and Miss Zhao and asked to go out to the house to see them.

"Just after our lunch, Mr. Thomas. Ivan loves ice cream. He said the one thing he hated about his life with the Chinese was that they had rice with every meal, after that first meal of oatmeal. Ivan wants ice cream, but I told him he needs to eat a hamburger first."

"That sounds pretty good. Can I come along?" the Agent said.

Liz drove Agent Thomas and Ivan out to the house after lunch. They arrived at the house to find that a few things had changed. Where there was once a bare backyard, there was now a swing set, which had been provided for the house by Social Services. The house also now showed signs of life. Where the hallway and entranceway were once quiet and clear, children were laughing and playing together, and there were toys everywhere. Liz had requested social services to buy the swing set and as many toys as their budget would allow.

"They seem quite normal," Agent Thomas said to Liz when they entered the house.

"Maybe now," said Liz. "You should have seen them a week ago. I doubt they will ever forget the abuse they endured, but we need to try. I just don't know what we can do about Olga."

"Who's Olga," Agent Thomas asked Liz.

"She's the little Moldovan girl. The only way we even know her name is from files we found in that Majestic Modeling business."

"I'd like to talk with the two adults if we could. I want

to hear their story in their words. I believe Ivan told me the truth, but I need to hear it from them as well."

"You understand that Chu Hua Zhao does not speak English, right?"

"Yes. No problem. I will watch her reactions as Hu Yang translates. I can see a lot in a person's face as they speak, even in another language."

"Thanks, Agent Thomas. I've also noticed the emotions on her face when I have Hu ask her a question. I'll bring them in now."

As the agent spoke with Hu, Liz noticed Agent Thomas's doubts slowly disappearing. When he asked Hu why he didn't try to stop Radovich from selling the girls for sex, Hu told Thomas that he truly believed that Radovich could harm the girls, even kill them, if they did not cooperate. He had seen Radovich beat the Moldovan girl one day when she refused to go with him. Hu and Chu Hua had decided to tell the girls to use meditation to ignore the abuse and pain, and that they would try to find a way to stop what was happening. Hu said that when the Police came to their door that day, he knew that their prayers had been answered.

Occasionally during their conversation, some of the children would run into the room with a toy, asking Hu or Chu Hua questions. At first, Hu looked afraid, thinking that Agent Thomas might be mad about the interruption. But Thomas would reach toward Hu and say, "No problem. Go ahead and talk to them."

Liz watched Agent Thomas as Hu talked with the children

and saw the look in his eyes. Liz could see that the agent was now seeing the good in Hu and Chu Hua.

After nearly an hour of conversation, Agent Thomas told Hu, "Please, tell Chu Hua that I am sorry that an American has done this to you and your children. We can never make bad things disappear, but I will recommend to my superiors that we must try to make all of you happy again if that is possible. I'm sorry for all the suffering, but I can see that the children love and respect both of you."

Agent Thomas asked Liz to find Ivan. Thomas shook Ivan's hand and thanked him. Ivan said, "No, thank you for believing me." At that, Liz saw Agent Thomas start to tear up and he gave Ivan a good hug.

"How can a human being have treated these children like this?" Agent Thomas asked Liz on the drive back to Erie. "I'm ashamed that an American has done this to these children. I saw that Moldovan girl, Olga, sitting in a corner when we left. She just kept rocking back and forth, staring at the wall. I've seen animals in the zoo doing that, and Radovich did that to her."

"That's why I don't sleep well at night, Agent Thomas. My fiancé worries about me, because I can't get these images out of my head."

"Liz, please call me Will. And I hope I can call you Liz."

"Yes. Of course."

Agent Thomas continued. "You have my word that I will recommend that the deportation order be revoked. I watched the children interact with Hu and Chu Hua, and there is no way they could talk to them like that if they thought those people had been the ones to harm them. Thank you so much for contacting us. I would feel terrible if these people were sent back to China."

"Thank you, Will. Now I need to find a way to settle them somewhere. I think Juvenile Services could use some Chinese oversight in trying to find good homes for those children. I think I've found a good foster home for Ivan, but first, I need to convince Roberto's wife that having a fourth child is a good idea. I just don't know what we'll do with Olga. She will need serious therapy for the rest of her life."

"Who is Roberto, may I ask?" Will Thomas asked.

"If you have time before heading back to Pittsburgh, I can introduce you. He works next door."

22

Burt's Apology

Burt knew that he owed Lucy and her friends an apology because his plan to get Cecil arrested had not worked out as he had hoped. He wondered if Cecil would ever get his just rewards for being a predator, and he owed those three ladies an explanation. He called Lucy and found her excited about what she, Natalie, and Maggie had discovered. They were about ready to contact Burt themselves.

"Burt, we have a couple guys for you to meet."

"Just say where and when. I'll be there," Burt answered.

Lucy and Natalie were sitting in the outside dining area at the Yacht Club when Burt arrived. They had two young men with them, in their early twenties, well dressed, but looked like they had lived hard for their age.

Natalie said, "Burt, meet Mario and Sammy. They were in my class back in high school, and they still live in my old neighborhood. We see one another occasionally and they

UNDERCOVER AGAIN - FIGHTING HUMAN TRAFFICKING

know I tend to tow-the-line, and I don't ask what they're into. Understand?"

"I get it. I guess I also don't need to know. Right?" Burt responded.

"You got it, and I told Mario and Sammy you could be trusted," Natalie continued.

"If they can help us with our problem, I'm all ears. My plan I suggested to my friend at the DEA got shot down," Burt said.

"I thought you were biting off more than your friend would accept. Am I right?" Lucy asked.

"Right. He had other ideas but said my plan was too risky. He didn't want to lose his job, he said. Pansy ass!"

"Well, I thought you were expecting too much when you suggested the idea. But back to why I asked you to come, I saw Mario one day when I was visiting my mom," Natalie said. "We started talking and Mario said he'd heard about me seeing Cecil. He wanted to warn me about something, to be sure I didn't get hurt."

Mario said, "Just so you know, Burt, I've always had a crush on this girl. She has her sight set higher than mine, but I don't want to see her get hurt. Understand?"

Natalie said, "You know that if you dropped your shady businesses and got a real job, Mario, I could change my mind." Burt could see the mutual respect between them as they smiled at one another.

"Okay, you two. Enough flirting in front of Burt," Lucy chimed in. "Let Sammy and Mario tell us about Cecil."

"Sammy has delivered some supplies to this Hendrickson

guy, you know?" Mario began speaking. "He always keeps a few relaxing agents for his guests, as he calls them. He told Sammy that after one of his guests went ballistic on him during his '*play time*,' he uses the white stuff to calm them down ahead of time."

Burt said, "I understand that you fellas don't want to use the words that might get you into trouble. No problem. But to be sure I understand, Cecil uses coke or other relaxers before he has sex with his guests, to be sure they cooperate. No need to answer if I'm correct."

There was no answer. "You got it right, Burt," Natalie said. "Lucy and I think it was that little thirteen-year-old who went ballistic on Cecil, so now he just drugs them first. He's a sick bastard as we see it. Right guys?" Natalie looked at her friends and asked.

They all nodded.

"We may do some things on the other side of the fence, Burt, but Mario and I respect women. Our mothers raised us to respect our sisters, girlfriends, and women in general. What we learned about Cecil bothered us, and because Mario knew that Natalie had been seeing Cecil, he wanted to warn her," Sammy said.

"So, we've been watching Cecil when he's on his boat," Mario added. "Sammy saw him bringing some girls aboard whom he recognized from our neighborhood. One of them was Margaretta Armato."

"From the Armato family, I'm thinking...?" Burt asked.

"The same," Sammy said.

"How old is Margaretta?" Burt asked.

"Fifteen maybe, but no more than sixteen. I know her older sister, who is only eighteen," Mario said. "So, Sammy called me and asked what I thought. I went to the marina and waited until Cecil's boat returned. He ushered the two girls out onto the pier and then Cecil left. We could tell that the girls were really spaced out. I know Mr. Armato, and I respect their family, so we decided to take the girls home. We explained to Mr. Armato where we found his daughter and that she seemed disoriented, so we were worried about her. We didn't tell him about Hendrickson, but I think his daughter told him the rest of the story later.

"What do you think will happen?" Burt asked.

"If Hendrickson raped Mr. Armato's daughter, he'll be beyond sorry. You don't mess with their family," Mario said.

A week after his meeting with Mario and Sammy, Burt got a call from Liz, she sounded rattled. "You didn't do anything to Hendrickson, did you?" she asked him without the usual greeting.

"No. Why?" Burt asked.

"He's dead. They found him on his boat out in Lake Erie. There was some kind of explosion. I just want to be sure you didn't do something that'd get you into trouble."

"No. I don't kill people, Liz. I might want to, but I tend not to go to that extreme."

"Okay," Liz said. "I'll let you know what the police and Coast Guard find out. I can't say I'm sorry, but I was hoping we'd punish him for his escapades with these girls."

"Maybe this was his punishment, if my guess is right," Burt said.

"What does that mean?" Liz asked.

"We both may not want to know," Burt replied.

Later that week, Liz called Burt again with new information regarding Hendrickson's death.

"The Coast Guard called in a fire expert, Burt. They had originally thought the explosion was caused by a propane grill on the back deck, which was full of food, even though it looked like Cecil was alone on his boat. The fire expert found that Cecil was locked in his cabin, using a steel bar to prevent the door from opening. He also found that the interior of the cabin had been doused with an accelerant, presumably gasoline. The grill didn't cause the gasoline to ignite."

"So, Hendrickson was murdered? Is that the finding?" Burt asked.

"Yes," Liz continued, "but here is the weird part. They performed an autopsy and, hear this, he was castrated before the fire started. Can you imagine?"

"It makes me shudder, Liz. But it couldn't have happened to a better guy. Like I told you during our last phone call, this may be his punishment for abusing those girls."

"I think you know more than you're telling me, Burt. Are you sure you weren't involved?"

"Trust me, Liz. I'm as surprised as you are, but maybe Cecil finally crossed some invisible line, and he got what he deserved. Do the police have any leads?"

"They say it's an ongoing investigation. But the lead investigator told me the fire burned away any evidence, and there were no witnesses. Nobody even saw or heard the explosion."

"Then, I can only hope his killers are satisfied, and the investigation dies as well," Burt said.

"I'm still hearing too much, like you know something that I don't, Burt. Need I worry?"

"Are you sorry that Hendrickson is dead, Liz? If I assure you that I was not involved, will you stop worrying?"

"I'm not at all sorry. I'll stop badgering you, Burt. Sorry."

"And are you going to tell the girl's family? I think they should know."

"Yes, but not the gory details," Liz replied.

Burt hung up with Liz and called Lucy. He didn't get into details but told her to let her friends know that justice had been served.

23

Burt - Nosing Around

A few weeks after his last visit to the hotel bar, Burt went back to speak with his friend, Fred, the bartender. Burt had promised to keep Fred informed about why he was so concerned with Cecil Hendrickson and the new guy in town who was handing out "entertainment" cards.

"It wasn't long after I last saw you, Hendrickson's yacht blew up. Were you involved in that?" Fred had a big smile on his face.

"I wish I could take credit for that, Fred. It's just not my style. I'd rather have seen him in jail, but maybe he finally messed with the wrong people."

"I wondered about that. I see a lot of teenage girls roaming the marina, talking to the boaters. It worried me that Hendrickson might be preying on them. Some of those girls come from good families who could pay to have that done. The scuttlebutt is that this was a hit, not an accident."

"You just might be right, Fred," Burt said with a big grin.

"Gotcha," said Fred. "I'll ask nothing further. So, what brings you down to my den of iniquity now that Cecil is history?"

"Just curious if you've seen any more from our ENTERTAINMENT card fella," Burt said

"I'm glad you mentioned him. He was here a few nights ago and got into a verbal battle with someone at the bar. I had to ask them both to leave. I haven't seen either of them since that night. If you remember, I overheard some guy asking Hendrickson how young he was looking for. Well, this guy, the other night, a different guy, said he wanted a refund because the girl he got wasn't a virgin like he'd been promised."

"Oh, hell! I need to get the cops after that S-O-B. He's dealing with kids, too," Burt said.

"That's why I kicked them out. Heads started turning as the other customers heard the subject matter. I can't report this stuff to management if I want to keep my job, Burt. But seeing that I know your feelings on the subject, may I call you when I see or hear things like this?"

"Please do, Fred. I'll report this to the right people and keep your name out of it.

Liz called Burt that afternoon to ask if he could meet with her and Tom Pierson at the DA's office the next morning.

"Sure thing, Liz. Something new?" Burt asked.

"No, it's actually about that ENTERTAINMENT guy. The FBI is interested, because of the claim that the girls are from Eastern Europe."

"Good timing, young lady. I just got some additional info about that guy. I'll share all the details tomorrow. So, it has been more quiet than usual. We haven't been meeting at all those crazy places lately. What have you been up to?"

"Just spending time with my fiancé, making up for all that time I was in a funk," Liz said.

"Is that an announcement? Did Steve ask the question?"

"He asks a couple times a week, Burt. It's just that I'm getting tired of telling him I'll need to think about it."

"Why are you terrorizing that poor young man, Liz? You can never find anyone who wants you more than Steve."

"I know that. Steve isn't the problem. Until recently, I was worried that I would make his life miserable with my moods. When I'm working on a heart-wrenching case, I get so involved that I take it home with me. Recently, working with these young Chinese and Moldovan kids was so emotional, I thought I'd snap. But Steve saw it happening, and he helped me through it. I had always kept those problems inside, but Steve talked me through that dilemma, even suggesting people to call and how to talk to the kids who knew some English. I now realize that Steve can be part of my life, and my problems don't upset him, as long as I include him in the process."

"You've got a keeper there, Liz. When are you going to break the news to him, so that he can stop asking?"

"I'm thinking tomorrow is the day."

"Maybe down the road, Steve can help you with new ones as well. You and I both know that you'll stick your nose into more of these cases. It doesn't look like trafficking will disappear any time soon," Burt said.

DISTRICT ATTORNEY'S OFFICE

"I spoke with Tom yesterday morning, before I called you," Liz said to Burt the next morning, after meeting him at the reception desk. "He told me that the FBI also has numerous leads and complaints about that fella who gave you the ENTERTAINMENT card at the bar. So, Tom asked me to contact you and ask if you could meet with the FBI agent in charge of that investigation. The police are also getting complaints about the guy who approached you in the bar. Normally the State Police would be involved, but the fact this guy is advertising a house full of Eastern Europeans, the State guys thought it best that the FBI take the lead."

"Sure thing, Liz. I'm glad you asked me to attend," Burt said.

"I met with Agent Herb Griffith just after we spoke yesterday. He wanted to hear first-hand about your experiences with this guy."

Liz led Burt to Tom Pierson's office, and the receptionist ushered him in. They were just about to start a casual conversation, when Tom said, "I think I hear Agent Griffith out front. If you don't mind, I'll let Liz handle this between you and Griffith. Liz will keep me informed, as necessary. But unless there are charges filed in Erie, we are just cooperating with the FBI in their investigation."

"I understand, Tom. As long as I know this guy is going to be stopped, I'm satisfied," Burt said.

"Thank you, Mr. Pierson. I'll let you know what is decided," Liz said.

Liz and Burt went out to the reception area and met Agent Griffith, and then headed to Liz's office. Griffith was barely into his 30's, very handsome and fit. Not a bodybuilder, but certainly athletic. His youthful looks made Burt wonder how qualified he might be.

Herb Griffith may have noticed the doubt on Burt's face, because once in Liz's office, he immediately started describing his training and experience. "You may wonder why the FBI sent me to Erie to follow up on this lead. As I told Miss Trent yesterday on our phone call, I checked on her background and experience before calling her. I was impressed by her undercover work with the Kentucky State Police, and I'm also aware of her recent inside work on the Majestic Modeling case."

"I'm the first one to say how qualified Elizabeth Trent is, but...," Burt started.

"I understand, Mr. Snyder. I mention Miss Trent's qualifications to emphasize that age is not always an indicator of someone's qualifications or abilities. When I first saw Miss Trent's picture in our files, I might have thought she was too young and inexperienced, but then I read her resume. Miss Trent is probably the most experienced sex-crimes investigator I have ever met, based upon her successes."

Liz broke in, saying, "Don't take offense, Herb. I think Burt is just concerned. He takes these cases as seriously as I do. And just call me Liz, please."

"Thanks, Liz. But let me tell Burt that the FBI has used me in similar undercover operations, such as Liz has done. Of course, I have played the male roles, such as a prospective buyer of trafficked women, a pimp if you prefer to call them, and occasionally as a 'John,' to get some pimp to sell me a woman for the night. I then use the information I've gathered, so we can close them down and build a case against them."

"And how many such operations have you worked on, Herb?

"I started right out of college, at age 22. I'm now thirty-two, and I typically work on five or six major cases a year and advise on others. Enough to satisfy you, Burt?"

"I'm sorry, Herb. I've had some bad experiences with the FBI, and maybe I still have a chip on my shoulder."

"I checked your background out as well, Burt. I understand. But just so you know, there are still some people in the Bureau who thought highly of your get-it-done attitude, and they still respect you. They just knew it would never work in the long haul, but they know you are a serious, dedicated man."

Liz then said, "I hope we've settled that. Are we okay now, Burt?"

"Certainly, Liz. I'm sorry. And my apologies to you, Herb, for jumping to conclusions."

"I'm used to it, Burt. And I'm sure Liz has had similar reactions."

"That's how I met my fiancé, as a matter of fact," Liz said.

"Fiancé? You finally said yes?" Burt nearly screamed.

"It was time, so yes. But we'll cover that later," Liz answered.

"Congratulations!" Herb said.

"Thank you. But let's have Burt tell you about this guy we

are calling the ENTERTAINMENT man, so we can decide how to proceed," Liz said.

Burt described his conversation with Fred, including the reference to young girls made to Cecil Hendrickson, and the recent dissatisfied customer, saying he had paid for a virgin, causing both men to be asked to leave the bar.

Herb said, "I could just call the phone number on that card, but that could raise suspicion. I also understand that there have been complaints from other bars and restaurants, so this guy might be wary of a phone call from someone he hasn't met. I'm wondering if we could do a little barhopping, Burt. Hopefully, we might run into this guy making his rounds, and you could introduce me as a prospective customer."

"I think you're right. We could start with the bar where my friend kicked him out. He may not want to go back there, but Fred may know where else the guy has been hanging out. Fred knows most of the bartenders in the Erie area."

"Can we start tonight, Burt? If he's had several dissatisfied customers, he may just move on to a new locale. Then I'd have to find his new location."

"I agree. The sooner, the better. Where are you staying? I'll pick you up."

"I'm at the Best Western. What time?"

"How about five-thirty? We can eat dinner at the bar, and talk with Fred," Burt said.

"It sounds like you two have a plan," Liz said. "I'll fill in Tom when I meet with him later."

"Thanks, Liz. And tell Steve I'm happy that you finally came to your senses," Burt said.

"I'm sure Steve agrees with you. We'll invite you over to celebrate one of these days."

"Plan on it," Burt said.

"Thank you, Liz," Herb said. "And congratulations on the engagement."

Herb Griffith was waiting at the door when Burt pulled up at Best Western. On the way to see Fred, Burt asked Herb, "I've been wondering, since I met you today, why your parents named you Herbert. I like the name, but Herb is not a 21st Century type of name. Just curious. I hope you aren't offended."

"Not offended at all, Burt. First, I was born and raised in Pittsburgh. A very conservative town would be an understatement. My Uncle, who's also my godfather, is named Herbert. They named me Herbert Adrian Griffith. I figured the Adrian name, if I used it, would have other problems. Being a 'jock' named Herb made me sound tough, whereas Adrian may have attracted more girls, but also would have caused the other guys to terrorize me."

"Understood. A good-looking guy named Adrian might have got you into a few fights. And now the big question. Whatever got you into the sex crimes division at the FBI?"

"That's what a lot of people wonder. It's sure not the Elliot Ness image, is it? Well, this is where life got serious for me when I was in middle school. I was too young to date, but I was sweet on a cute 13-year-old girl in my class. My parents said, 'no dating 'til you're fourteen,' but I knew Della would be my first date. That summer, Della disappeared. The police said she ran away from home, but I knew her well, and she was happy at home. Her parents were good people, she wasn't being abused, and she had no reason to run away. Six months later, she was found on the side of a road in Tennessee. She was alive but had been nearly beaten to death. She recovered physically, but she has never been the same mentally. I tried to visit her, but her parents refused. I found out several years later that she had been kidnapped, sold to a sex-for-sale stable in Tennessee, and had been repeatedly raped. Despite the drugs they used on her, she refused to cooperate, so they beat her and dumped her, thinking she was dead."

"Oh my God, Herb. I'm so sorry. Terrible for her, but I can't imagine your trauma, having a friend endure that. She still has problems coping?"

"Yes. I finally saw her when I was eighteen. She wouldn't look me in the eyes and told me to leave her alone. I tried several more times, but she'd just scream at me to go away. She still lives in the old neighborhood with her parents, and if she sees me when I'm visiting my parents, she crosses the street or turns around to walk the other way."

"Those people killed her, emotionally, didn't they?"

"Exactly. Della's dad said they might have done her a favor to have finished her off. Della was their only child, and she is an emotional vegetable, despite being alive. So, now do you understand why I take joy in stopping and prosecuting these animals?"

"Very much so. And I'll do anything necessary to help you get this guy," Burt said.

"Thanks, Burt."

"How would you like me to introduce you to Fred, by the way."

"Can you trust Fred not to warn this guy, Burt?"

"Oh, yes. Fred is the one who first expressed concern about him and brought him to my attention. He overheard the reference to young girls, and it bothered him enough to tell me about that conversation."

"Then quietly tell him I work in law enforcement, and I'm investigating the guy. Just don't say FBI right now."

Fred was surprised to see Burt so soon after they met the day before. Burt saw the confusion in Fred's eyes and said, "I told you I knew who to call, Fred. But truthfully, the law was already hearing complaints all over town, and this guy showed up. So, Fred, I'd like you to meet Herb." Leaning forward, Burt continued, He's with the law, investigating that guy who was handing out those cards."

"Oh, good," Fred said. "I was hoping he'd not been forgotten."

Herb reached over the bar and shook Fred's hand. "Thanks for being concerned, Fred. I understand that one operator was recently closed down, and now this guy is trying to take his place. Let's stop him quickly, and maybe the word will get around to stay away from Erie."

"I agree, Herb. I found out on Sunday that my granddaughter knew one of the girls who was abused in that last operation. We need to stop these people."

"So, tell me. Have you seen this guy recently? The one handing out cards?" Herb asked.

"Not since he got into that scuffle with the customer in

here. But I've heard he's still around. I understand he's hanging around the bars downtown instead of the waterfront hotels since he got in trouble here. I also heard he doesn't hand out those cards anymore. I overheard one of the customers say that he'd called that number, and it had been disconnected," Fred said.

"I thought the card was not something a seasoned professional would do. They don't want their contact information to be tracked down. I checked that number as well and even tried to track the billing address. It was at a UPS Post Office box, which has also been closed. The name was false as well," Herb said. "The lady at the UPS Store said the guy came in and paid cash. He is probably an upstart, and the prices he'd been quoting showed he was an amateur."

"Wow," Burt said. "I didn't realize that you'd really done your homework on this before you came. Impressive."

"Burt, take him up to the Metro for dinner. Talk to Tommy behind the bar. I'd love to have you stay for dinner, but he won't come back here."

"You're a good man," Herb said. "Thank you for your cooperation, Fred."

"Burt knows I have no stomach for these guys. Just let me know when he's out of business, That's the only reward I want."

"I'll have Burt tell you once we close the case. Deal?" Herb said.

The Metro was one of the old, classic bars that still had a hotel in operation. Most of the old hotels closed once the big, waterfront hotels opened. Burt told Herb he had met

Tommy, the bartender, but didn't know him as well as Fred. Burt suggested that they order dinner and sit in the bar, watching for the man who Burt had met.

Walking into the bar, Burt was surprised to see the 'Entertainment' man, sitting with four others at a corner booth. He told Herb, "Damn, if he isn't here. The guy in the light blue button-up in that back booth. He's obviously changed his tactics, talking to a group like that. When I saw him, he only talked to guys sitting alone."

"He's just learning. He's fishing right now. Talking guys' BS. Those that keep mentioning girls, he'll single them out later. He learned that giving cards after a five-minute conversation just caused him trouble. Now, he'll learn who's serious and who's not. Seeing we've located him, Burt, and before he recognizes you, I'm going to have you leave. Understand? I'm going to find a way to get into that conversation over there. No offense, but sneak out before he spots you. I'll call you tomorrow."

"I like your style, Herb. I'm outa here. Later." And Burt left, keeping his face turned.

24

Herb - Hunting

Herb knew his job better than his colleagues ever suspected. He went up to the bar, ordered a cheap, scotch on the rocks, took one sip, and walked up to the table of men. He just stood and listened nearby, trying not to look as if he was eavesdropping. When he heard the conversation slow a little, he walked over and said, "Are you guys from Erie? I'm finding it very boring compared to back in Pittsburgh. I know there must be things to do around here, but I haven't found them yet. Any advice?"

One of the men said, "Well, to start with, have a seat. We are split between Cleveland Brown fans and Pittsburgh Steelers fans here. I assume you're a Steeler fan?"

"Yes, of course. And I'm also a fan of the Steelerettes. The Browns never had cheerleaders, right? How can you watch football without watching those tight cheerleader uniforms?"

"Well, a true football fan doesn't need cheerleaders," one of the Browns' fans said.

"But when the team has a bad season, we've got the girls," Herb said, licking his lips.

Herb stayed at the table and continued talking for a while, but then thanked them all for the friendly banter and said he'd be moving on. He finished by saying, "Go Steeles, and thank you for the distraction of the Steelerettes." The guys all laughed as he left.

Herb went to the bar, asked for a refill of his drink, and sat at the far end of the bar. As he suspected, the guy in the blue shirt kept watching him, and after about five minutes, he got up and headed toward Herb.

"I don't think we ever asked you. What brings you to Erie? I'm Robbie, by the way."

"I'm Herby. This is my first trip, but I represent a foundry in Pittsburgh. We hope to be selling castings to some of the manufacturers around Erie. I'll be visiting quite often. That's why I'm hoping to find some amusement in town."

"What do you consider amusement? No sports except college stuff, and certainly no Steelerettes."

"College girls are all too stuck-up for my taste. Not looking for a wife either. Tried that once and never again."

"So, you're looking for female companionship, but no strings?"

"Yeah, but I'm not looking for some dirty old hag, either."

"I know a guy who has a house full of young Russian girls. All clean and any age you want."

"Interesting. But I'm on a tight budget. Probably can't afford it."

"Hey, you're on an expense account, right? You can bury

some of it in travel expenses. If you're happy, tell your boss you'll sell more castings."

"I must admit, this makes Erie look better. How much?"

"You're looking for a young one, I guess? He charges $150 an hour, but if you want an all-nighter, the cost per hour is less. These Russian girls are all willing to please. They know what American guys want."

"Any way I can choose one? I don't want to have a girl come to my room and not be happy with the merchandise if you know what I mean?"

"I don't think he normally does that, but seeing you might be a regular customer, maybe he'll allow it."

"I'm over at the Best Western, room 312. I'll be there until ten tomorrow morning, then probably back by three, after I make my factory calls. Let me know what the guy says. I hate to spend time with a girl I haven't seen. Understand?"

"I got it. I'm sure I can work something out. I'll call you tomorrow, Herby."

Herb went to his hotel. He was surprised that he made so much progress this quickly. He was pretty sure the guy was working alone, and his referring to someone else to gain permission was just a ruse. He may be using one of the older girls as his '*bottom*', like a house mother. If his stable was truly Russian, or other Eastern Europeans without a passport, they had nowhere to go if they ran, so they were easier to control. Herb was hoping to get to the actual house where he kept the girls, but he didn't think he'd be that lucky.

The next morning, at about nine-fifteen, he was eating his free breakfast in his room when the phone rang. "Herby, this is Robbie. The boss man says he'll let me take three girls to some parking lot, and you can choose. How long do you want her to stay?"

"I was hoping for all night. I have $600 for this trip, but what if I don't like the three you bring? How many girls does he have? Can't I see them all?"

"All night is usually a grand. Maybe I can meet you at the parking lot, show you the girls, and if you're not satisfied, I can bring three more. But those six are the young ones. The rest are older, which you may not want."

"That should work, but what about the price? I don't have a grand to spare on this trip."

"I'll take the $600 this trip, but only six hours. Next time it's $750 if you want eight hours."

"Okay, Robbie. That sounds fair. Where can I meet you? Does around nine-thirty sound alright?"

"Do you know where the zoo is, south of downtown? I'll meet you by the entrance, in the parking lot. It's closed at night, but easy for you to find. Have your money along. I'm doing you a favor, knowing you'll be a regular."

"Thanks, Robbie. You'll see a lot of me if this girl works out."

"Okay. Nine-thirty then. See you there."

Herb called the FBI Field Office in Pittsburgh and talked to the Special Agent in charge of Victim Services. He told the Agent that his headway on the Erie case developed quickly, and he needed support that evening to tail the suspect. He expected their office would not respond that quickly, and he knew the Special Agent was familiar with Burt Snyder. Herb said, "Can you authorize Burt Snyder to tail the guy? I've got this trafficker willing to deliver three girls to a remote location, and he'll need to return two of them to his house. I need someone to tail him who won't be noticed. You know that Burt is good. Can we use him for this quick job?"

"I'll have to run it by the agent in charge, but I think he was also a Burt supporter when Burt worked in Youngstown. You call Burt and see if he'll take the assignment, and in the meantime, I'll take the request up to the front office. I assume this tail could be the key to closing a case quickly, am I correct?"

"It sure could," Herb said.

"Okay. That's the way I'll present it to him. Let's hope he's in a good mood today. I'll call you back."

Herb called Burt and filled him in on the events after he'd left the prior evening, and the surprising agreement with Robbie that morning. He asked Burt if he would accept a short assignment for the evening if the Pittsburgh agent in charge would agree.

"Of course, I'd accept. If we can find those girls and close down his operation this quickly, it'd be great. Once you know where the girls are located, who will make the raid? You don't have enough agents in Pittsburgh."

"My next call is the State Police Detachment, here in Erie. I know they have access to the Crisis Unit, and we'll need immediate support for the girls we find. Robbie says he has ten girls, but he could be bluffing me some, to make himself look better than he is. I still think this guy is an amateur who worked for someone else. When he heard that Radovich and

Majestic were gone, he decided to break out on his own. He probably purchased a few girls from his old boss and pays him a percentage of the girls' income."

"It still amazes me that these guys operate as if it's a legitimate business," Burt said.

"Sure. If one guy is good at recruiting, or he has a good bottom girl that recruits, he gets over-stocked for his area. He then makes deals with other pimps to sell his overstock. These trafficked girls mean no more to them than cars in a used car lot. Hey, Burt, I see an incoming call from my office. I'll call you back. Thanks."

Herb answered the call, and it was the agent in charge, John Savage. "Are you telling me you have a chance to close that case this quickly, Herb? You just got to Erie a couple of days ago."

"Looking good, boss. I think this guy is new to the business. He agreed to deliver several girls so I could choose. If he has to return the others to his stable, I need a good man to tail him."

"Well, I remember Burt Snyder. He wasn't cut out for the Bureau, but he was one of the best surveillance guys I've ever seen. Is he still dressing like a bum? He couldn't convince the agent in charge at that time, that surveillance in a black car, wearing a dark suit and a red tie, was not the way to do it."

"Yes. I was shocked at first by how he dressed, even at a meeting. And you're right about the car as well. I saw him in a rusty old Toyota yesterday, and he told me he owns seven old cars, which he changes daily when he's working," Herb answered.

"Seeing I have nobody available on such short notice, I can justify using a private guy, particularly when he's someone so familiar with Bureau procedures. If you close this case early, Washington will never question my decision. So, go ahead, if you're sure you can nail this down."

"Thanks, Mr. Savage. I didn't want to stretch this out in case the perp started to get suspicious. If he called one of his suppliers, they'd tell him not to trust me so quickly."

"Keep me informed, Griffith. And who will be making the raid once you locate his stable?"

"I was just preparing to call the local State Police Detachment when you called. I'll ask for their assistance tomorrow, and I'll ask them to have a couple of people from their Crisis Team to help with the rescues," Herb responded.

"Sounds like you've got everything covered, Griffith. Great job! I hope it all goes well."

Herb then called the State Police and spoke with a Sergeant who seemed very aware of the complaints from the local hotels about some guy pimping girls at the bars. He said, "I knew the FBI had been informed, but we thought it might take weeks, even months, to get a response. So, you're saying you're already close to a raid?"

"I'm tailing this pimp tonight, hoping to pin down where he keeps the girls. If this pans out, I'd like to make the raid tomorrow morning, in case the perp gets suspicious. Can you have a couple of members of the Crisis Unit on hand, as well as three or four Troopers?"

"I know the Lieutenant would love to get these complaints

settled, so I'm sure that he'll agree. He's in a meeting right now, but I'll call you back in thirty minutes. Sound good?"

"Thanks, Sergeant, I'll wait for your call," Herb said.

Herb called Burt again to confirm that Burt had been okayed for the tail operation that evening. He told him that John Savage had been complimentary about Burt's surveillance skills.

"I remember working with John a few times. We always got along. He warned me that the agent in charge back then... I think it was a guy named Phelps... was not happy with my ideas. I'm glad to see that Savage was promoted."

"So, I'm meeting Robbie at the entrance to the zoo at nine-thirty tonight. What else do you need to know, Burt? I'm not sure why he picked the zoo for this."

"That area is quite open and well-lit. He's probably making sure that someone like me won't be able to hide. I know how to hide right out in the open. But if you go into the parking area near the entrance, I can spot him when he pulls in. When he pulls out, I'll know it's him. There won't be any other cars there at that time of night. I'll call your cell once I start the tail. But what are you going to do with the girls? If you don't choose one, won't he get suspicious?"

"But I do plan on choosing one. I'll take the one who looks most frightened, and I'm going to tell her what's happening. Then I'll talk to her at the State Police Detachment."

"Might I suggest that you ask Liz Trent to help with that? That young girl may be frightened and refuse to talk with you. But Liz has a way with these girls, putting them at ease."

"But this isn't a District Attorney's case at this point. Will she be able to get involved?"

"Liz will certainly ask for Tom Pierson's permission, but Tom considers Liz to be his expert on trafficking cases. I'm betting that Tom will allow Liz to help you."

"Thanks, Burt. I'll call her."

Herb now called the District Attorney's office and asked for Liz Trent. Liz answered the transferred call and asked, "How is the investigation going, Herb?"

"Much better than expected, Miss Trent. That's why I'm calling."

"It's Liz, remember? So, what do you need, Herb?"

"Thanks, Liz. Here's what happened since we met on Wednesday." And Herb went on to explain his being lucky, running into Robbie on his first night of barhopping, and being able to convince Robbie to bring three girls for him to choose from. Also, he explained the idea of having Burt tail Robbie back to his location.

"That was a great tactic, Herb. Congratulations!"

"Maybe just lucky. I also think that this guy is an amateur. A seasoned pimp would never have agreed with my idea. But seeing it appears to be working, I have the State Police lined up for a raid tomorrow morning, including some Crisis Team personnel to work with the rescued girls. But I have one problem, and Burt suggested I ask for your help."

"Oh, yes. I almost forgot. Where do I come into this?" Liz asked.

"You may need to ask Mr. Pierson, but I do plan on choosing one of Robbie's girls tonight. I wanted to interview her at the State Police Detachment, but Burt thought that might frighten the girl, and she'd refuse to talk. Burt suggested that you might help with talking to her."

"I will need to ask Mr. Pierson, of course. This certainly isn't a local case without any of those complaints resulting in official charges. I doubt if Tom would object, as long as I'm not introduced as an Assistant D.A. When do you expect to need me, and where?"

"I meet Robbie tonight at nine-thirty, so I'm thinking about ten o'clock at my hotel. Burt also thought the State Police Detachment would be frightening. What do you think?" Herb asked.

"I agree with Burt's assessment. I'll call the shelter where we placed a few of the girls we rescued from the motel over in Ohio. I'm sure they'll let her stay there overnight. But initially, why don't I meet you at your hotel? I'll be in the Lobby, and the girl probably expects you to be taking her to a hotel, so she'll stay calm."

"Wonderful. So, as long as Mr. Pierson agrees, you'll meet me in the Best Western Lobby at ten tonight?"

"I'll be there early. I'll find a secluded spot so we can talk initially. Then I'll tell the girl that we're taking her to a safe house with other girls. I'll call the shelter right now."

"Thank you so much, Liz. I hadn't thought through this aspect of the operation. It wouldn't be right to have the poor girl in a holding cell."

"Glad I can help," Liz said.

25

Burt - On the Tail

About eight-thirty that evening, Burt parked his oldest car, a very rusted-out Dodge, across the street from the entrance to the zoo parking lot. Burt flagged down the first Erie Police car he saw on the street, and he handed the officer one of his business cards. He told the officer he would be at that location on surveillance for an hour or two, with his hood up. He told the officer he could check him out with the desk sergeant on duty if he felt it necessary.

The officer responded, "No, that's not necessary, Mr. Snyder. You're well-known in the department, and I've only heard good things about you. I can just leave you alone, or if you need my assistance, just flag me down again, or call the Dispatcher. I'd love to know what's going down. Can you tell me?"

"I can't tell you now, but you have my card, so call me in a few days. I'm sure I'll be able to tell you once the investigation is complete. And thank you for the offer to help. So, if you see some unusual traffic in and out of the zoo parking lot in the next hour or two, can you please ignore it? I can assure you the zoo animals are safe."

The officer chuckled and said, "No problem, Mr. Snyder. Great to meet you in person."

When the officer left, Burt raised the hood on his car and sat on the curb-side fender, appearing to be waiting for assistance. At around nine-twenty-five, he saw Herb Griffith's rental car enter the zoo parking lot. He then saw a car pass by the lot slowly, with several people in the car. Burt stuck his head under the hood and tried to look concerned. The car turned around in a service station up the street and returned, pulling into the zoo's parking lot. Burt dropped the hood, got into his car, and parked in the nearest cross-street, so he could pull out to follow when Robbie came out. It took about ten minutes, and Burt saw the same car coming out of the zoo. This time, Burt could recognize Robbie's face as he went by, lit by the business sign across the street. Burt got a good look at the car, an older Jeep. He waited until Robbie was nearly one block away before pulling out. He followed as far behind as he could and saw Robbie turn and head out 38th to an older subdivision. On those side streets, Burt shut off his lights and watched Robbie's Jeep pull into the garage of an old home. Burt waited about fifteen minutes to be sure the car was there, in case Robbie was just making another delivery. Then Burt drove by, writing down the address. He pulled up the street and turned, watching the house. About twenty minutes later, he saw Robbie back out of the garage, and one woman came running out to the car, jumped in, and they took off.

Burt decided to tail Robbie again, and he followed him to a hotel. He dropped the woman at a side door, and she knocked. Someone opened the door and let her in, and Robbie drove away. Burt took different streets back, but when he drove by Robbie's house, he saw Robbie just closing the garage door. Burt figured this would be helpful information for Herb's investigation. Burt continued following Robbie's deliveries one more time, to a different hotel, and then considered that he didn't want to be recognized and left the area.

Burt had promised to call Herb once he had the location, which he did. He told Herb that he saw Robbie make two deliveries to two different hotels after he followed him back, so he knew for sure that he had found the stable location. Then he asked, "Did all go well at the zoo?"

Herb said, "All is well. Liz is here with me, and we are speaking with Miss Lorena, from Bulgaria."

"That's wonderful. Call me when you need that address. It's less than ten minutes from the zoo. That's why he chose that location. I think he had a busy night."

When Herb walked into the hotel Lobby, he could tell that the desk clerk seemed surprised that he was accompanying a young woman, very overdressed, and looking like she was very underage. Robbie had brought three girls to the zoo as he promised. Two appeared to be about sixteen, and this girl, looked more like fourteen, and she was very shy, almost frightened. Herb could see that Robbie was surprised that he chose the one he did because she was not as good-looking as the other two. However, he told the girl to go with Herb, and Herb handed over the $600 agreed upon.

Then Robbie said, "I'll pick Lorena up at your hotel in the morning. I know I said six hours, but I'm busy tonight. I'll pick her up at eight o'clock. Be a nice guy and feed her breakfast, would ya?"

"No problem, Robbie."

With that, Robbie hurried the other two girls back into his car and left.

Herb didn't talk to the girl much during the drive to his hotel. When he asked her to put on her seat belt, and reached over to help, he saw the girl flinch. She was scared, so Herb figured she was quite new in Robbie's stable.

Entering the Lobby, the girl looked very confused, like Herb had done something she hadn't expected. When Herb led Lorena towards Liz, sitting in the breakfast area of the Lobby, Lorena still looked confused, but Herb saw some relaxation when she saw that Herb was leading her toward a young woman. Herb wondered what crazy, even disturbing things this young woman had already experienced in her young life.

Herb motioned for Lorena to sit near Liz and said, "Lorena, I'd like you to meet Liz. She wants to help you."

Still looking confused, Lorena said, "Robbie did not say we were playing group games."

"No, Lorena," Liz said. "You are not going back to Robbie. We will help you now. You do not have to let anyone use your body anymore."

"But Robbie will send me back to Bulgaria. I must earn money to become an American citizen."

"That's not how it works, Lorena," Herb said. "Robbie

would never let you become a citizen. He was keeping all that money for himself."

Lorena started to cry, and Liz tried to comfort her. "We will take you to a safe place with other girls. We can't promise, but we will try to find a way for you to stay in the United States. But for now, you are not going back to that house."

"What about my sister?" Lorena asked. "She is at the house."

"All of the girls will be rescued in the morning. Your sister is also there?" Liz asked.

"Yes, she is only twelve. I need to protect her. I ask Robbie not to send her to hotels, but he has started to send her."

"She will be with you tomorrow, and neither of you needs to do these things anymore," Herb said.

Herb looked over at Liz while Lorena was crying, and he quietly mouthed, "Twelve?"

Liz just nodded, as tears started in her eyes.

Herb told Lorena that she should go with Liz. She would be staying in a home with other rescued women, and her sister would be with her tomorrow. Liz patted Herb on the back and led Lorena out of the hotel with her arm around her shoulders.

As Liz and Lorena left, Herb saw relief in the desk clerk's eyes. He had probably suspected the worst.

Herb called the State Police Detachment and told the desk sergeant that he was to notify the Lieutenant that the pimp was coming to the Best Western at eight the next morning. He asked for two State Troopers and two Crisis Center personnel to be at the hotel around seven o'clock and park in the back. Herb said they would meet and plan the next step.

Herb then called Burt back and told him how much he appreciated having Liz with him to talk with the young girl, he told him she had a 12-year-old sister with her at Robbie's stable.

Burt gave Herb the address and how he had followed Robbie to a couple more deliveries, just to be sure he had found the actual location where the girls were kept. Burt said, "Maybe the Bureau will want to look into the insiders at these hotels. They're meeting the girls at the side doors to avoid suspicion. Those girls would not be walking through the Lobby of a nice hotel, unaccompanied, and the 'Johns' don't want to be seen with them either."

"Thanks, Burt. Please put those hotels and experiences in your written report. I may be back to follow up on those myself. As John Savage told me, you're one of the best surveillance guys he's ever seen. You've now proved that to me."

"Tell John I said Hi, and you guys let me know if I can be of further help."

"Will do, Burt. I'll see you again, I'm sure."

Next, Herb called Liz to find out how things had gone with Lorena. Liz told him that Lorena had cried throughout the drive to the women's rescue center. "She's very worried about her sister," Liz told Herb. "But I was glad to see that Beth was still at the center. Beth is one of the older girls found at the raided motel in Ohio. Beth seems to hate the fact that these young girls are being recruited into 'the life', and she had a serious talk with Lorena, telling her she'd be happier to get out, and that Lorena and her sister would be safe.

"I'm just worried that INS may just send them home. They weren't happy in Bulgaria, and sending them home, after what has happened, will make them outcasts in their society. I'll discuss this with Burt. He has a friend whose mother knows some good immigration attorneys, and maybe they can look into helping some of these girls.

"This has been the toughest part of the cases I've seen here in Erie. The girls from outside the United States are at the mercy of the INS. I know that the Immigration guys have their job to do, but sending people back to China, Central America, and Eastern Europe, after these traffickers and pimps have messed up their lives, just seems criminal. We'd be sending them from one hell they've experienced here, back to another hell in their native countries."

Having heard the stories, plus the worries about deporting these women, Herb had a hard time sleeping. He woke up well before his five o'clock wake up, and was waiting for the breakfast buffet to open at six.

At six-forty-five, two uniformed State Troopers and two plainclothes personnel, one woman and one man, walked into the lobby. Herb saw them and walked over to them, showing his ID. They quickly introduced themselves, and then Burt gave them a quick synopsis of the last few days. He described Robbie and told them he was coming to the hotel to collect the woman that Herb had rented for the evening. Because they already knew the location of the stable, Herb figured it would be better to arrest Robbie while he was alone, here at the hotel, and then head to the stable location.

Herb said there could be as many as ten, possibly more women at the location, and he wanted them taken into protective custody, but not arrested. One of the girls was a 12-year-old sister of the girl that Herb had chosen the evening before, who had stayed at the women's rescue center overnight. Herb asked the woman officer to take special care of that 12-year-old, explaining that they were taking her to see her sister.

"I understand," the officer said.

At eight o'clock, Herb saw Robbie's car pull into the parking lot. Robbie sat in the car, probably realizing it was going to be difficult to retrieve his girl through the busy lobby. So, Herb asked if one of the Troopers would be ready to stop Robbie's car if he decided to leave. That Trooper left out the back door and positioned himself in an unmarked car near the parking lot exit.

Finally, Robbie got out of his car and entered the lobby. He saw Herb in the breakfast area and started in that direction, then saw the other trooper heading to block the front door. Robbie tensed as if to run. That's when he saw Herb flashing his badge, followed by the two plainclothes officers. Robbie hung his head in disgust. "I should have known. Everyone told me not to trust a new 'John.' Damn it all!"

The officers led Robbie out the front door, patted him down, cuffed him, and read him his rights. They then got into their cars. When Robbie saw all the cars heading toward his street, he asked Herb, "How'd you do it? I didn't see anybody on my tail."

"I'll never tell. He's the best."

During the drive, Herb called Liz to tell her they had Robbie and would be at his stable in a few minutes. Liz said, "Have the Troopers take the girls to the women's rescue center. This little lady sitting next to me is anxious about her baby sister."

At Robbie's house, which turned out to be owned by his grandmother, now residing in a Nursing Home, Herb said, "I think you should just cooperate and open the front door. Tell the girls they are not being arrested, just being taken to a safe house. They can take some personal belongings, but only essentials. We'll have the police return and collect their things for them. And please point out Lorena's little sister. This lady officer is going to take special care of her."

Robbie did as he was instructed. One of the older girls seemed upset over what was happening, and Herb suspected that she was his bottom or house mother. The other girls seemed to show no emotion, but the 12-year-old was easy to point out, and the woman officer did a good job of explaining to her what was happening and that her sister was safe and waiting to see her.

Robbie was brought to the State Police Detachment for questioning. At first, he was refusing to speak, but then he said he wanted a lawyer but could pay. He didn't have enough money for an attorney because housing ten girls had cost him more than he had figured it would. Every one of his 'Johns' was bargaining with him on price. Herb offered to call for a public defender, and Robbie started thinking. "If I cooperate, can I get out of this?" He asked.

"Well," Herb said, "you were selling young teens for sex. What do you think?"

"But when I bought the five Russian girls, the guy said I couldn't get in trouble, because they weren't Americans."

"I can read the statute to you, Robbie. The law doesn't say you can sell foreign kids. They're protected by our laws as well. But where did you buy those five? You didn't bring them in yourself, I'm sure."

"I wouldn't know how to do that. Some guy in Philadelphia had too many. Just got them last month, but the Russians aren't big money-makers like the guy told me they'd be."

"You do realize that the two young girls aren't Russian, don't you, Robbie?"

"Sure they are. They told me they were from Bulgaria, and I know that's in Russia somewhere."

At that point, with that stupid statement, Herb realized that there would be no useful information to be gained from Robbie, and he told the State Police that they should just charge him.

26

Closing the Fake Daycare

Everyone involved with the Chinese children knew that the house from which Rudy Radovich had operated his human trafficking operation, was now closed. There was also the question of what to do with Hu Yang and Chu Hua Zhao. Liz had been working with them, but her other duties at the DA's office were keeping her from her desire to work with those kids. Then one day, Liz received a call from an Asian Cultural Center near Pittsburgh, which changed everything. They had heard about the rescued children, and several Chinese families in their area had expressed interest in adopting some of the children. The center said that they would have offered to take the children under their care, but they were very understaffed.

When Liz told the director of the center about Hu Yang and Chu Hua Zhao, everything started to fall into place.

Meetings were held with the Pittsburgh-based Asian Center and the local Erie Children's Social Services staff. Social

Services didn't want to send the kids back into an abusive situation, so they set up meetings with potential adoptive parents and planned to use Hu Yang and Chu Hua Zhao to meet, translate as needed, and "approve" any matches with prospective new parents.

Liz had heard about the women's rescue center from her work at the D.A.'s office. The center catered to women and children escaping domestic violence situations. When Beth and Lexy were rescued at the Ohio motel, Liz asked the director of the center, if the two girls could stay at the center until the State Police Crisis Unit was able to decide how they could be handled. The director had told Liz that Beth had been counseled by several of the women victims who stayed there, and Beth asked to stay. Lexy, on the other hand, thanked the center's director but told her she could never live a *'square'* life and had found a friend in Cleveland who wanted her to work there. When the director asked what kind of work, she wouldn't answer. Beth later told the director that Lexy missed the excitement of 'the life' and was probably going to live with a pimp again.

When Liz needed a place for the Chinese girls and the one Moldovan girl to stay, waiting for their INS decision, the center again agreed to house the girls temporarily. The older women were very helpful in caring for them, but the big surprise was Beth. Beth seemed appalled by the abuse the young girls had endured, and she paid special attention to them, without being asked. She played with them and even comforted them when they cried. Then Liz was able to have those girls returned to Radovich's house, under the care of Hu Yang and Chu Hua Zhao.

The center's director asked Beth if she wanted to take classes as a counselor, and Beth enthusiastically agreed. Therefore, when Liz brought the Bulgarian girl, Lorena, into the center, Beth took her under her wings and talked to her. Although Liz understood these women and their history of abuse, she had never been trafficked herself. Liz could see that Beth made an immediate connection with these young girls because she had personally gone through many of the same experiences in her own life.

Liz said, "Beth, I can't thank you enough for being so kind and understanding with Lorena. You seemed to have put her at ease immediately."

"Miss Trent, I had no idea that the men who did this were using such little girls. When Lexy and I went to Rudy's motel job, we knew what we were doing. I didn't like it, but Lexy did. But it was our decision, and it was our way to get away from our fathers. But these little girls were stolen. They were forced to have sex. Some of them cry every night."

"It's terrible what they've had to experience," Liz said. "I'm so grateful that you're here to help them. As you can see, very few of these girls choose 'the life' that you and Lexy chose. But even the two of you wouldn't have chosen it if you were happy at home with your parents. You're now seeing these girls from other countries, who were kidnapped, but some American girls are also kidnapped into 'the life' and are not there by choice. Once they've been in that life long enough, they're afraid or ashamed to go home, so they don't even try to escape."

"I'm glad I can help these young ones," Beth said. "I remember some of the older girls out at the motel, like Brenda. I think she was about twenty, and she'd been tricking since she was twelve, she had told me. I heard she went looking for another guy to take her in because she didn't ever want to go '*square*' again. I think she's the one that called Lexy to go to Cleveland."

"Are you tempted to go back, Beth?" Liz asked.

"I was at first. I had gotten used to it but was still upset with the guys who got rough. But now that I see what happens to these young kids, I actually hate those men. I'm taking some classes so I can become a better counselor, but I've told the director that the classes are too clinical for me. The counselors don't have real experience, and that's why those girls want to talk to me and trust me."

Liz said, "You have a lot to offer here, Beth. If you finish high school, I can help you get into counseling classes at the University, and you can tell your Sociology professors how to change their textbooks to better help rescued girls. Don't let anyone tell you that you can't change the way things are done, because you have the inside track on how it should be done."

"Thank you, Miss Liz. I thought I had no way to leave 'the life', but since you brought me here, I feel hopeful."

"I'm happy for you," Liz said. "If you ever feel tempted to leave and go back, just look at how much good you can do by helping these girls. You can always call me if you need a pep talk. Nothing in life is always perfect, so don't get discouraged if you have setbacks."

Beth laughed. "I don't want to go home, and the sex in that place was not what I thought it was going to be. I like it here and hope I get to stay."

"I'll have to get the Department of Social Services to agree, but with the problems you had at home, I know they won't make you go back there. I'll tell them what a wonderful job you're doing here."

Now that Liz had settled the Chinese children and Hu Yang and Chu Hua Zhao with the cultural center near Pittsburgh, that left Ivan and the girl from Moldova. Liz was having difficulty placing the girl. According to the director of the women's shelter, the girl was disruptive due to her constant chanting and swaying. It was 'upsetting to the other children,' she said. As much as they felt sorry for her, there was nothing any of them could do to help her. In fact, the last time Liz had seen her, the girl was swaying back and forth in what is called "the zoo animal sway."

Then a few days later, Liz got a call that would change everything. The Director said she had been called into the room where the Moldovan girl was, only to find her sitting relaxed against Beth as Beth calmingly soothed the girl with words telling her she was safe, and that everything was going to be okay now. Even though the girl most definitely didn't understand any of the words Beth was saying to her, there was something in Beth's tone that seemed to have worked.

Liz rushed to the center, hoping to see this with her own eyes. When she got there, she went up to Beth and quietly said to her, "You are the first one to be able to comfort this poor girl. How did you know to do this? We've all tried to reach out to her, but no one has been able to do it."

Beth looked up and said, "I think she can feel, that I have suffered too. She trusts me. Do you know her name?"

"Majestic's records have her listed as Olga," Liz said.

"Miss Liz, would you ask Ivan if he would help me talk to her?" Beth asked.

"Ivan has tried before, but let's bring him in," Liz said.

Liz went out to get Ivan, he was playing with some of the older children in the airy, fenced-in courtyard.

Ivan sat on the floor next to Beth, and Beth said, "Please tell her that my name is Beth. I want to be her friend. What is her name?"

Ivan translated Beth's words into the Moldovan/Russian dialect, and the girl looked up at Beth's face and quietly said, "Linnea."

Liz suddenly remembered the nude pictures in Radovich's files, in a folder named 'LINNY'. It was the girl that was being fondled, her body tense and her fists clenched tightly. She had been living with that fear and tension for a long time.

Beth told Ivan, "Tell Linnea that I will take care of her. I have suffered too, and I understand."

After Ivan translated, Linnea reached up and put her arms around Beth's neck. She quietly cried on Beth's shoulder. Everyone in the room teared up, including young Ivan.

Liz looked at the picture unfolding before her and felt a weird feeling. If this was Linnea, then who was Olga?

Liz was determined to find out, so she approached Beth

and whispered in her ear, asking her to tell Ivan to ask Linnea if she knew another girl named Olga.

Linnea perked up at the name Olga. "Did they find my sister?" she asked Ivan in Moldovan. Ivan translated this to Liz and Beth, who then asked the girl when she last saw her sister.

"Miss Liz thought that your name was Olga," Ivan said to the girl. "Where is your sister, Linnea?"

"Olga is under the flowers at the big house," Linnea replied.

Ivan immediately understood what this meant and told Beth.

Beth and Liz gasped when the weight of Ivan's words sank in. Liz was able to get Beth to get Linnea to talk about her sister, Olga. After Liz heard what she needed to hear, she called the State Police and told them what she had learned. The police returned to the 'big house' as Linnea called it, and carefully dug up the flower garden behind the house, which Linnea had mentioned. There, they found the badly decomposed body of a young girl, estimated to be about 13 years old. An autopsy revealed the cause of death to be several blows to the skull and face, causing serious fractures.

When Liz heard that the police had found Olga's body, she cried. She could not believe that Rudy would beat a young girl so senselessly simply because she "tried to argue with Rudy," according to Linnea's account of what led to the beating. Olga had tried to prevent Rudy from sending Linnea off to be with some of his male clients when Rudy became very upset and hit Olga in the face, causing her nose to bleed. Linnea kicked Rudy in the legs when he did that, and that's when Rudy hit Linnea very hard, causing her world to turn black.

When she came to, Olga was nowhere to be found. She heard noises in the back yard, and when she peeked out the window, she saw Rudy digging a hole in the flower garden. Then she saw Rudy throw Olga into the hole and fill the hole with dirt.

Liz asked Ivan to ask how long ago this was, and Linnea told Ivan, "Maybe three months before you came to the house."

Liz eventually compared Ivan's timeframe with the decomposition determined by the autopsy, and the times closely agreed.

With this new information, Rudy Radovich was charged with First Degree Murder. That trial is pending.

27

Elisa Jandra

Liz visited Beth and Linnea regularly at the Rescue Center. During one such visit, Beth asked Liz about the little girl she had seen at the motel. Liz knew she was referring to Elisa. The Jandra family was the original reason why Liz became involved in the human trafficking problem in Erie. She had kept in constant contact with the family since becoming involved. And now that the perpetrators of these heinous crimes were beginning to drop like flies, Liz had been more than willing to deliver some good news to them, at the urging of Burt When Mr. Jandra had heard how Cecil Hendrickson had died, he smiled satisfactorily.

Mrs. Jandra was also satisfied that Lenny Simpson was remorseful. Elisa, on the other hand, was having trouble letting go. The family had met with Lenny and their two counselors, hoping it would help, but it had not. Instead, in that meeting, Elisa confronted Lenny with an icy stare and silence.

"There are some things in life that an apology cannot get

forgiveness for," Roberto had said to Lenny when he saw the confusion in the boy's eyes. "Elisa gave you her answer, and you need to accept that."

When Liz heard about Elisa's trouble with opening up again, Liz called Mrs. Jandra and asked her if would be willing to allow Elisa to meet with Beth, one of the workers at a local women's rescue center. She told Mrs. Jandra how Beth had been able to get another girl talking successfully, and how that talking had led to solving the murder of the girl's sister.

Mrs. Jandra agreed, so Liz suggested having Elisa come to the rescue center.

Liz called Beth and told her that Mrs. Jandra had agreed to the meeting, and Beth said she was nervous, but looking forward to it.

The day that Elisa Jandra and her mother arrived at the rescue center to meet with Beth, it took all but fifteen seconds for Elisa to recognize Beth. She ran to Beth and hugged her. "You were always nice to me," Elisa said.

Beth began to cry and kissed Elisa's neck. She said, "I'm so sorry."

"Why are you sorry?" Elisa asked.

"Because I couldn't stop it," Beth said.

"You did what you could. Thank you," Elisa said.

The two women looked at one another and left the three girls to talk. "We will never understand, but those two are bonded by having shared hell," Liz said.

After Beth and Elisa shared lunch, they continued talking. Finally, Mrs. Jandra came in and said, "Elisa, I think we should be heading home now."

"Oh, Mom. Can't we stay a little longer?" Then she turned to Linnea, who had come in later, and introduced her to her mom. "Mom, this is Linnea, she was telling us stories about Bulgaria."

Beth said, "Well, maybe it's enough for today, Elisa. But you promise you'll come back? We have so much more to talk about."

"Can we, Mom? Beth and Linnea want me to help with some of the other girls who stay here alone. Do you think I could sleep over with them sometimes?"

"I'll have to check with the director on that, but I think that would be fine," Stephany Jandra said.

While the girls were hugging and kissing goodbye, Mrs. Jandra and Liz stepped a few feet away.

"My God," Stephany Jandra said when they were out of earshot, "I somehow have my little girl back." Liz smiled, noticing the tears welling up in Mrs. Jandra's eyes.

"It's wonderful, Stephany. But know that there will be setbacks. I hear that Linnea, even Beth, cries some nights. The nightmares may never totally disappear, but because these girls can share their inner feelings with someone who understands, they find comfort and survive." I don't fully understand it, but now you know it works."

"Thank you to both of you for making this happen," Mrs. Jandra said to Liz. Then, turning to Beth, who had since walked up with Elisa and Linnea in tow, she said, "Beth, know that I am eternally grateful. "

28

Liz & Steve

Liz went home that evening and talked to Steve about all of the events in their life which were finally falling into place. "Do you realize that in just over two months, Majestic Modeling's real operation was exposed, and Rudy Radovich is standing trial for Child Sex Trafficking and murder, the motel brothel in Ohio had been shut down, with help from you and Burt, Beth has hopefully left 'the life' for good and is happy, working at the women's rescue center. We found potential adoptive parents for the Chinese kids and full-time employment for Yu and Chu Hua. Having Lexy return to a pimp in Cleveland was disappointing, but we've had some wins, including finding the best youth counselor in existence, trapped in the body of a soon-to-be seventeen-year-old girl."

"And to make things even better, you're finally letting me into that part of your life," Steve said. "I can't tell you how happy that has made me, Babe."

"I must admit, it has helped me a lot to feel I can unload

all these things on you. I was afraid that you wouldn't want to hear all these bad things going on in my life."

"Can you now see that talking them over with me not only helps you but also helps me? We need to share both the good and the bad. I loved you either way, but now I feel that I'm part of your life, and I can help you, not just be an observer," Steve said.

"I do understand. I'm sorry it took so long for me to see it. When you talked me through the problems with how to handle the Chinese kids, and actually gave me ways to talk with Ivan, that Moldovan boy, I started to understand. I was trying to approach the problem too technically, and you approached it from just a plain human angle, talking to him as a 14-year-old boy. I heard the same thing from Beth, working at the Women's Center. She told me that the counseling training she was taking was too clinical, not personal. I was surprised that a 16-year-old understood that because a few weeks ago, I didn't."

I never got all the details about the ENTERTAINMENT guy, who had a whole house full of Russian girls. Give me those details, and then I'll share my news.

"Well, there were actually only five from Eastern Europe. That stupid Robbie, was telling his clients they were all Russian, but some of them were just Americans with Eastern European names, like Olga and Anastasia, who were born here. And of course, Lorena and her sister were from Bulgaria, which Robbie thought was part of Russia."

"What's going to happen with those girls that Robbie had?" Steve asked.

"The oldest one was twenty and was Robbie's girlfriend, though I think he was selling her for sex as well. She's being very uncooperative and is defending Robbie. She's trying to say that he was taking care of these girls, and if they had sex, they decided to do so. With testimony from both Herb, and Burt witnessing Robbie dropping girls at hotels, that defense won't hold water," Liz said with a laugh. "And three of the Americans have shown up on missing persons lists in the Philadelphia area, so they were abducted. Maybe they can be safely returned home if they have good family support."

"And those young, Eastern Europeans?" Steve asked.

"The FBI and INS are contacting Bulgarian authorities on those two. Lorena said their parents were dead, but we're not sure. It doesn't appear they wanted to come to the United States, so they were possibly trafficked out of some orphanage. The other three don't speak English, but Lorena thinks that two are from Romania and one possibly from Moldova. We'll need to see what the Feds find out about them. They look to be fifteen or sixteen."

"One last question, and then I have that news to share," Steve said. "Whatever happened with that boy, Lenny, and his visit to Mrs. Jandra?"

"I heard from Laurie Willis just last week. Roberto Arroyo has been amazed by the change in Lenny's progress. He seems to have taken responsibility for Elina Jandra's terrible treatment by Radovich and Hendrickson, and Mrs. Jandra has allowed Lenny to talk with Elisa. Elisa still has issues, but Lenny's apology and concern seem to have helped Mr. & Mrs. Jandra. They will never fully get over what happened to their daughter, but knowing that Rudy is going to prison and that Hendrickson met such a traumatic end, probably an assassination in reality, they at least feel like justice has been meted out. And then yesterday's meeting between Elisa and Beth at the Rescue Center was like watching a miracle occur in front of us. As Stephany Jandra said, 'She got her little girl back again.'"

"So, no real happy endings, but at least some of your perps have been stopped. Are you feeling a little better about life now?"

"Until the next one appears, I guess. But what is your news? Good news, I hope," Liz asked.

"Yes, it's great news. I called Mom & Dad to tell them that you finally found me worthy to agree to marry me, and..." Steve began.

"I hope you didn't tell them that way, or I may just change my mind, you jerk!" Liz said.

"No, but you know my mom has always wondered when you'd say yes. She even asked me one time if I was treating you right because you'd kept saying no."

"I've never said no, my love. I just said that I needed more time. That was my fault because I was afraid to involve you in my crazy life. Once I started talking to you about my issues, I realized that I was wrong. So, what did your mom say?"

"It was my dad who told me this good news. Now that Dad is pretty much running my uncle's construction company, he has decided they need a larger tug and barge. Instead of looking for another used one, my uncle told Dad to get proposals on a new build. He wants to visit Erie and talk with my boss at the shipyard, so they want to come over and celebrate our engagement, and help decide on our wedding plans."

"That's wonderful, Steve. When are they coming?"

"My mom has called your parents, and she now wants us to speak with your folks to see when they can come to Erie. Your parents' schedule is tougher, being college teachers, so Mom said that you should find out when they can come to Erie, and my parents can make it whenever your mom and dad can make the trip."

"That's exciting. Our parents have only been together for our graduations at the U-of-M, so this is a wonderful opportunity for them to get together. I'll call my folks tonight."

"One more thing," Steve said. "I got a call from Valerie, Linda's mother. She invited us to dinner, and she emphasized that it wouldn't be at Cracker Barrel. Did you know that Mr. Pierson had approved her work-study application? Valerie said she starts working for you next Monday, and she works half days while taking her classes at the University."

"Tom seems to have kept that bit of information a secret, but I couldn't be more pleased. Did she mention what Linda is doing?"

"Yes, she said Linda is still working for Mrs. Behrendt, and in addition to cleaning, she buys her groceries and runs other errands. Mrs. Behrendt is treating Linda like the granddaughter she never had, Valerie said."

"And yes, I almost forgot. We've been invited to a large celebratory dinner at the Arroyo household. Roberto said that after several weekends of Ivan spending time with the Arroyo family, Ivan has agreed to be fostered by the Arroyo family.

Roberto and his wife, as well as their three kids, all want Ivan to be part of their family, but they want Ivan to feel comfortable with them before they file for adoption. I love the way that Roberto has handled this, giving Ivan the freedom to choose. I'm sure Ivan will want and accept an adoption, but he knows it's his choice.

ABOUT THE AUTHOR

Bob Ojala is an author, writing both non-fiction and fiction books, generally dealing with life in the maritime industry. His novels center around real-life events where possible, changing names and locations to protect privacy.

Bob Ojala has a BSE in Naval Architecture & Marine Engineering from the University of Michigan. Bob spent four years in the U.S. Coast Guard, 17 years with the American Bureau of Shipping, and 8-1/2 years with the U.S. Army Corps of Engineers, in addition to 30 years in his own business (including the time while with the USACE). Bob is still active in marine surveying.

Bob is a Wisconsin native with Finnish roots. His father was a Merchant Mariner for 32 years, giving Bob his interest in the Maritime Industry, but not the desire to be a sailor.

Bob Ojala's books include:

- Autobiography of a Ship's marine Surveyor
- World Travels & Adventures of a Ship's Marine Surveyor (Autobiographical)

ABOUT THE AUTHOR

- Sweetwater Sailors (non-fiction, real-life stories from Great Lakes mariners)
- A Tugboater's Life (Contemporary Romance based upon Great Lakes Marine Construction)
- The Tugboater Family (stand-alone, but following characters from A Tugboater's Life)
- Crew's Ship Affairs (Life on a large cruise ship, BELOW the passenger decks)
- KIDNAPPED – A Tugboater's Tale (Human Trafficking in middle-America)

www.ingramcontent.com/pod-product-compliance
Lightning Source LLC
Chambersburg PA
CBHW070539010526
44118CB00012B/1177